THE PART-TIME VEGETARIAN'S YEAR

NOURISH

EAT WELL, LIVE WELL

THE PART-TIME
VEGETARIAN'S
YEAR

Nicola Graimes

FOUR SEASONS OF
FLEXITARIAN RECIPES

FOR MY MUM

THE PART-TIME VEGETARIAN'S YEAR
Nicola Graimes

First published in the UK and USA in 2020 by
Nourish, an imprint of Watkins Media Limited
Unit 11, Shepperton House, 83–93 Shepperton Road
London N1 3DF

enquiries@nourishbooks.com

Commissioning Editor: Daniel Hurst
Copy Editor: Emily Preece-Morrison
Managing Designers: Georgina Hewitt and Glen Wilkins
Production: Uzma Taj
Commissioned photography: Liz and Max Haarala Hamilton
Food Stylist: Valerie Berry
Prop Stylist: Linda Berlin

A CIP record for this book is available from the British Library

ISBN: 978-1-84899-381-5

10 9 8 7 6 5 4 3 2 1

Typeset in Gill Sans
Colour reproduction by XY Digital
Printed in China

Publisher's note
While every care has been taken in compiling the recipes for this book, Watkins Media
Limited, or any other persons who have been involved in working on this publication,
cannot accept responsibility for any errors or omissions, inadvertent or not, that
may be found in the recipes or text, nor for any problems that may arise as a result
of preparing one of these recipes. If you are pregnant or breastfeeding or have any
special dietary requirements or medical conditions, it is advisable to consult a medical
professional before following any of the recipes contained in this book.

Notes on the recipes
Unless otherwise stated:
Use medium fruit and vegetables
Use medium (US large) organic or free-range eggs Use fresh herbs, spices and chillies
Use granulated sugar (Americans can use ordinary granulated sugar when caster
sugar is specified)
Do not mix metric, imperial and US cup measurements:
       1 tsp = 5ml 1 tbsp = 15ml 1 cup = 240ml

nourishbooks.com

CONTENTS

Introduction   6

About this Book   8

The Flexitarian Kitchen   10

SPRING   16

SUMMER   60

AUTUMN   112

WINTER   156

Index   202

Acknowledgements   208

Introduction

How things have moved on since my original *The Part-Time Vegetarian* was published five or so years ago. The culinary climate has definitely changed for the better, with more of us choosing to eat plant-based meals on a regular basis. And to prove the point, research figures show that, impressively, one in three in the UK have cut down on the amount of meat they eat, with 60 per cent of vegans and 40 per cent of vegetarians having adopted their dietary preference over the last 5 years.

While the health benefits of a plant-based diet – the reduced risk of major chronic diseases, obesity and diabetes – are well documented, it has been the growing concerns over the environmental impact of intensive animal farming that has spurred much of the move towards flexitarianism, vegetarianism and veganism over the past few years. Recent research has revealed the hefty footprint of intensively reared meat, with the conclusion that the single most effective way to reduce our environmental impact is a global shift towards a flexitarian diet that contains only small amounts of ethically reared, good-quality meat and dairy, eaten once or twice a week with a plant-based diet being predominant.

For me, one of the most exciting aspects of the shift towards flexitarianism is how inspiring and creative plant-based cooking has become. Nowadays, no chef worth their salt would forget to include a vegetarian or vegan dish on their restaurant menu. What's more, many openly relish the exciting culinary possibilities of plant-based cooking.

As a family, we have become more mindful of what and how we eat over the years. Like many families our eating preferences vary and I'm constantly on the look-out for meals that both meet our differing tastes and that can be adapted if need be. Whether we eat meat just once a week; just at weekends; as part of an extended family get together; for a dinner party; or not at all, I've found that flexitarianism is a way of eating that can be moulded to suit our individual needs.

I'm hoping that this sense of versatility, adaptability and variety shines brightly in the recipes in this book. Importantly, vegetables always take centre stage with a focus on what's in season. Where meat (or seafood) are included they are in cost-, eco- and health-conscious small amounts and treated as a garnish, side, topping or second to the plant-based components of the meals. At the heart of this book is the growing relevance of a mindful connection with what and how we eat.

About this Book

In contrast to my first book, this one is organised by season, rather than meal type. With most fruits and vegetables now available year-round, it could be argued that we've lost touch with eating with the seasons, yet I have a gut feeling that we may see a gradual reversal of this in years to come as well as a move to eating more locally.

In this book the approach to the flexitarian part of the recipes has also evolved. To explain, many of the vegetarian (and often vegan) recipes come with a flexitarian or 'Part-time Variation', showing how to adapt it to include meat, poultry or seafood, if you wish. (It also means that you have effectively two recipes in one, so if cooking for both vegetarians and flexitarians the meal can readily be adapted.) The most crucial part of these variations has been to include the meat, poultry or seafood in modest amounts, so they become almost a garnish, topping, side dish or nifty, economical way to use up leftovers, such as a Sunday roast. I wanted to flip the outdated concept of "meat and two veg" on its head.

Plant-based ingredients are the foundation of every recipe, flexitarian or not. Where a recipe contains dairy, I've tried to give a vegan alternative – with vegetarian recipes it's all too easy to rely on dairy as a protein source. While some may ask why include meat or fish at all – and they have a point – the aim of this book is to show how easy it is to eat mainly vegetarian/vegan meals on a weekly basis.

In this book, you'll find recipes for starters, light meals and mains, with each dish being, as far as possible, a complete meal. So, there is always a protein and carb element, which means that you don't have to spend time considering side dishes. I'm also a big fan of including extras, such as a tahini sauce, raita, salsa, pickle or relish, to unify a dish and add another layer of flavour and texture, as well as boost the nutritional value.

Additionally, each chapter includes a special feature – a menu that centres on a seasonal gathering. You'll find a spring lunch to enjoy with friends or family, a summer barbecue feast, a picnic, an autumnal brunch, Sunday lunch fare, and a winter festive celebration.

Whether you are vegetarian, vegan or flexitarian, the core of this book is a celebration of seasonal fresh produce, with over 100 simple, nourishing ideas on how to enjoy eating with the seasons.

Eating Seasonally

Sharing an allotment with a group of friends over the past few years has opened my eyes to the beauty of eating with the seasons. With some fruit and vegetables pretty much available all year round in supermarkets, it's easy to become detached to what's in season. Yet, eating with the seasons means you get to enjoy fresh produce when it's at its peak; when it tastes its best; and when it's most readily available and reasonably priced due to the laws of supply and demand.

For the sake of simplicity, I've divided the book into the four main seasons. I know it's not always that cut and dried - seasons can meld into one another or be unpredictable; not all vegetables neatly fit into a particular season - the produce available in early spring can differ greatly to that later in the season, for example; and there are regional and national variations, too. However, these are small vagaries. This approach is also about the types of meals we fancy at each time of the year, from lighter dishes in the spring and summer to warming, heartier meals in the autumn/fall and winter, and you'll find this is also reflected in the recipes in each chapter.

Eating seasonally also means making the most of local produce with its reduced transportation and support for the community. Many of us, including those who live in cities, will have access to local schemes such as farmers' markets, greengrocers, street markets and box deliveries – even supermarkets are getting better at stocking seasonal, local fresh produce.

This is a positive and mindful way to eat. Far from being restrictive, eating seasonally can make us more creative in the kitchen and perhaps encourage us to try vegetables that we've ignored in the past. Each season brings with it a treasure trove of fresh produce to try. When testing the recipes, I was frequently surprised to find how well the various fresh seasonal produce complemented each other flavourwise – it's as though they were meant to be together.

WHERE TO BEGIN...

The beauty of a flexitarian diet is, as its name suggests, flexibility. There are no hard-and-fast rules, but the unifying dietary choice is that it's mainly plant-based. A recent study in *The Lancet* came up with the recommendation that we should be eating 50 per cent less red meat (other research sets the figure at 80–90 per cent) and doubling our intake of nuts, fruits, vegetables and beans/pulses.

Bearing this in mind, I've come up with a few basic guidelines to help. Vegetarians should ideally eat mainly from the 'Base your diet on...' list, right, with moderate amounts of dairy and eggs (vegans omit the dairy and eggs). Flexitarians who eat meat, poultry and seafood are recommended to eat mainly from the 'Base your diet on...' and 'Eat in moderation...' sections, with foods listed in the 'Eat rarely (if at all)...' section forming a limited part of the diet.

BASE YOUR DIET ON...
Fruits and vegetables
Beans and pulses
Nuts and seeds
Grains, preferably whole

EAT IN MODERATION...
Dairy: organic from grass-fed or pasture-raised animals
Eggs: organic free-range

EAT RARELY (IF AT ALL, IF VEGETARIAN/VEGAN)...
Meat: organic grass-fed or pasture-raised animals
Poultry: organic free-range birds
Fish: wild-caught from sustainable sources – look for the MSC-certified blue label
Shellfish: from sustainable sources – look for the MSC-certified blue label

The Flexitarian Kitchen

When a vegetable is in season, it's most likely to be at its tastiest and cheapest, which is a perfect time to get ahead and freeze or chill for the coming week, reducing food waste in the process.

Making the most of the freezer

Considering my freezer is usually packed, it's reassuring to know that a full freezer costs less to run than a half-empty one, so it pays to make the most of this invaluable space. Other than stocks, soups, stews, curries, puff pastry and pitta bread, this is what you're likely to find in my freezer:

Egg whites: stored individually in small lidded pots or ice-cube trays (marked with the date). Egg yolks can be frozen too, but it's best to beat them lightly with a pinch of salt first, as they can become gelatinous after freezing.

Wine: remnants of red and white wine to use in sauces, risotto, gravy and stews.

Citrus zest: if a recipe calls for orange, lime or lemon juice, don't throw away the zest. To prepare, before juicing finely grate or cut the zest into shreds, then open-freeze on a lined baking sheet. Transfer to a zip-lock freezer bag once frozen. Only use the zest from unwaxed fruit.

Bread: use up any slightly stale bread by blitzing it into crumbs, then freezing in freezer bags. Use the crumbs straight from the freezer and add to vegetable or nut roasts, rissoles, or fry in olive oil until crisp and golden to make a crunchy topping for pasta and salads or *pangritata*.

Herbs: if you grow herbs, it pays to freeze them for the winter months. Sturdy herbs, such as sage, rosemary, bay and thyme, freeze better than those with delicate leaves, such as basil and parsley, which are better used in cooked dishes after freezing. Place on a lined baking sheet, open-freeze and transfer to a zip-lock freezer bag once frozen. Kaffir lime leaves and sticks of lemongrass are also economical to buy in bulk and freeze.

Fruit: berries, especially at the peak of summer when they're plentiful and cheap to buy, are ideal for freezing for future use and they can be used straight from frozen as an added bonus. Open-freeze raspberries, strawberries, gooseberries, blueberries or fresh currants in an even layer in a baking tin, then transfer to a zip-lock bag once frozen. Rather than wasting browning bananas, I often freeze those that are at the stage of being over-ripe and mushy. Remove the skin and place the banana in a lidded container or bag before freezing. They make a very nice banana ice cream when blended with yogurt, crème fraîche or cream, or add to smoothies and cakes. Cooked orchard fruit such as apples, pears, cherries and plums freeze well and are great for turning into sauces, compotes or adding to pies and tarts.

Vegetables: bags of frozen peas, leaf spinach or broad/fava beans are an indispensable source of green veg when needed. They make excellent sauces, soups, purées and fritters and are a great way to add colour, nutritional value and flavour to stews, curries, pasta, rice or grain dishes. Gluts of fresh produce, such as tomatoes, green beans and courgettes/zucchini, can also be frozen. It's best to blanch beans and courgettes/zucchini first, then refresh under cold running water before open-freezing on a lined baking sheet. Tomatoes can be quick-frozen without blanching and are best for sauces, soups or stews. Chutneys, pickles, ferments and relishes are also perfect for using up seasonal produce.

Grains: cooked rice, barley, freekeh, farro, wheat berries and bulghur wheat all freeze well and can be a great time saver or a perfect way to extend the life of grains if you cook too much and have leftovers – they'll keep 2–3 days in the fridge but up to 3 months in the freezer. If freezing, make sure the grains are cool after cooking, then freeze flat in zip-lock bags straightaway. Thaw grains in the fridge or more quickly at room temperature or in a microwave – you have to be particularly careful with rice, which shouldn't sit around for too long at room temperature and should be reheated thoroughly until piping hot. I like to use cooked rice in pilafs, egg-fried rice, arancini, or spiced rice; barley is great in soups and stews; while other grains add substance to salads or as a side dish.

Beans and pulses: dried beans and pulses are more economical to buy than canned – although they do need some forward planning. It can be useful to cook up a batch: soak the beans overnight in plenty of cold water, then drain and rinse. Place in a large pan, cover generously with cold water and bring to the boil. Allow to boil for 10 minutes, then reduce the heat, part-cover with a lid, and simmer for 1½ hours or until tender. Drain and leave to cool, then freeze in portions.
To use, defrost slowly in the refrigerator so the beans keep their shape.

Staples

I've limited this list of staples to my must-haves... it has the potential to be huge, but these are a few of my favourite storecupboard essentials:

Oils: coconut oil; olive oil (extra virgin); sesame; good-quality sunflower or cold-pressed rapeseed oil and ghee.

Vinegar: raw, unfiltered apple cider vinegar; red and white wine vinegar; balsamic; rice vinegar.

Sauces: mirin; miso paste (brown and white); tahini; soy (light and dark); chilli sauce; English and Dijon mustard; peanut butter.

Dried ingredients: pasta; noodles, udon, soba, egg, rice; mushrooms, porcini, oyster and portobello; seaweed, dulse, nori, wakame and mixed seaweed for salads.

Grains and pulses: polenta/cornmeal; quinoa; spelt; gram/chickpea flour; black rice, brown rice, jasmine rice, sushi rice, risotto and paella rice; canned (and dried) chickpeas/garbanzo beans, butter/lima beans, cannellini, black beans, haricot; Asian fermented black beans; lentils (puy, beluga, split red, green and brown).

Nuts and seeds: walnuts, chestnuts, cashews, pistachios, almonds, hazelnuts; sunflower seeds, sesame (white and black) and pumpkin seeds.

Spices: chipotle chilli (dried, powdered or flaked); Turkish pul biber; chilli/hot pepper flakes; smoked paprika; nigella seeds; cumin; coriander; harissa; ras el hanout; sumac; cardamom; cloves; turmeric; star anise; shichimi togarashi.

Others: vegetable bouillon/stock powder; nutritional yeast flakes; capers; olives; sun-dried tomatoes.

Don't throw away...

Leftover bread, wine, egg whites... but what about making the most of the lesser-loved parts of vegetables? Vegetable peelings, outer leaves, gluts and leftover cooked vegetables all have their uses, with the latter a perfect way to up the veg content of a frittata, tortilla, fritter, soup, hash, salad or dip. I'm a big fan of vegetable purées – cauliflower, leek, onion, broccoli and carrot – to serve as a side sauce or dip. Steam your vegetable of choice and blend with a little bouillon powder, hot water and cream – easy.

Root vegetables: potato, carrot and parsnip peelings make perfect crisps. Toss them in sunflower or olive oil and roast in the oven until crisp and golden. Drain on paper towels and season before serving. Root vegetables also make the perfect base for a vegetable stock/broth with onions and celery, peppercorns and bay leaf. Cover the root veg with water and simmer over a low heat for about 45 minutes before straining. Carrots, cabbage, celeriac/celery root, beetroot/beet and parsnips can all be turned into healthy slaw with a dressing of mayo, crème fraîche, Dijon mustard or lemon juice.

Cauliflower: the outer green leaves are just as delicious as the pale white florets. Toss in oil and roast until just tender. Any leftover florets can be grated raw or lightly cooked into rice and grain dishes, or used to make a tart or pizza base.

Beetroot/beet leaves: if you're lucky enough to have the leaves attached when buying raw beetroot/beets, lightly steam them as you would spinach and serve as a side veg with a squeeze of lemon juice and a drizzle of olive oil. Alternatively, use in a tart/quiche or add in the latter stages of cooking a curry or stew so they keep their colour and nutrients.

Cabbage: sauerkraut and kimchi are obvious choices for leftover cabbage. For a speedy version of kimchi: mix together 1 handful of shredded Chinese cabbage, 2 thinly sliced spring onions/scallions, 1 shredded carrot, 1 finely chopped red chilli and 2.5cm/1in thinly sliced piece of fresh root ginger with 4 tbsp rice wine vinegar and 4 tsp caster/superfine sugar and ½ tsp salt. Stir well and leave at room temperature for 30 minutes to let the flavours develop. Eat immediately or store in an airtight container in the refrigerator for up to 1 week.

Broccoli stalks: in my eyes the best bit. Slice the stalks and add to stir-fries, soups or toss in oil and roast or steam. Try blending the cooked stalks and florets into 'broccomole' with avocado, garlic, lime juice and chilli. Delicious.

Cooked pasta/rice: I've touched on ways to use surplus cooked rice on page 12, but if you've leftover cooked pasta, leave it to cool and store in an airtight container in the fridge for up to 3 days (or freeze for up to 3 months). Use in frittatas, tortillas, bakes or as a base for a salad.

Cooked beans: if cooking dried beans it pays to make more than you need to turn them into humous, burgers, fritters, purees or mash, or add to soups and stews.

Parmesan rind: use to add extra flavour to soups, stews, pasta sauces or risotto – remember to take it out before serving.

Spring

A time of renewal and rejuvenation, spring marks a period of new growth, shoots and leaves. It is peak season for asparagus, watercress and purple sprouting broccoli, which are a welcome distraction from the root vegetables and brassicas of the harsher winter months. In the same vein, the types of dishes we typically enjoy at this time of year shift from the warming, comfort food of winter to lighter, uplifting dishes as we welcome longer days and a steady rise in temperature.

Seasonal vegetables:

Asparagus (peak)

Beetroot/beets (in season)

Broad/fava bean (in season)

Brussels sprout (in season)

Cabbage, green (peak)

Cabbage, red/white (in season)

Carrot (in season)

Cauliflower (peak)

Cavolo nero (in season)

Celeriac/celery root (in season)

Chard (in season)

Garlic (in season)

Globe artichokes (in season)

Greens (peak)

Kale (peak)

Leek (peak)

Lettuce (in season late spring)

Onion (peak)

Onion, spring/scallion (peak)

Potato (peak)

Potato, new (peak)

Purple sprouting broccoli (peak)

Radish (in season)

Rocket/arugula (in season)

Samphire (in season late spring)

Shallot (in season)

Spinach (in season)

Sweet potato (in season)

Turnip (in season)

Watercress (peak)

Rejuvenating coconut and spinach broth

~~~~~~

With brighter days and lighter evenings, spring spurs a craving
for more uplifting meals that reflect the new season. I'm hoping
this will give you a real spring lift after the fug of winter. It's loaded
with good things, such as ginger, turmeric and chilli, and plenty
of seasonal veg. To give the broth extra flavour-infusing time, you
could make it up to 2 days in advance, then leave to cool and store,
covered, in the fridge – although this isn't essential.

Serves **4**
Preparation time: **20 minutes**,
plus standing time
Cooking time: **35 minutes**

875ml/30fl oz/generous 3¾ cups
    good-quality hot vegetable
    stock
7cm/3in piece of fresh root
    ginger, sliced into thin rounds
6 kaffir lime leaves
2 large lemongrass stalks,
    crushed slightly with the blade
    of a knife
1½ tbsp light soy sauce
2 bird's-eye chillies, deseeded
    and thinly sliced
250g/9oz flat udon or soba
    noodles
350g/12oz asparagus spears,
    woody ends trimmed
sesame oil, for brushing
400g/14oz can coconut milk
1 tsp ground turmeric
4 large handfuls of baby spinach
juice of 1 large lime
sea salt and freshly ground black
    pepper

To serve
2 spring onions/scallions, thinly
    sliced diagonally
1 handful of coriander/cilantro
    leaves
1 tsp black sesame seeds

Put the stock, ginger, kaffir lime leaves, lemongrass, soy sauce and
half of the chilli in a large saucepan and bring almost to the boil, then
reduce the heat to low, cover with a lid and simmer for 20 minutes to
infuse the stock with the flavourings. (This can be done in advance
and the broth left to infuse until ready to serve. It will keep in the
refrigerator for up to 2 days.)

Cook the noodles following the package directions, then refresh in
cold water and set aside.

Meanwhile, brush the asparagus with sesame oil. Heat a griddle/grill
pan over a high heat and chargrill the asparagus for 8–10 minutes,
turning occasionally, until charred in places and tender. You may
need to cook the asparagus in batches. Set aside.

While the asparagus are chargrilling, strain the broth, then return
it to the pan with the coconut milk and turmeric. Reheat the broth,
then add the spinach and cook for 2 minutes or until tender. Add the
lime juice and season with salt and pepper, to taste.

To serve, divide the noodles evenly between 4 large shallow bowls.
Ladle over the coconut broth and top with the asparagus, the
remaining sliced chilli, spring onions/scallions, coriander/cilantro
and sesame seeds.

. . . .

PART-TIME VARIATION

Rejuvenating chicken or beef broth Replace the vegetable stock
with chicken stock, made from the bones of a roasted chicken, or a
beef bone broth.

Leek and white bean soup
with roast garlic oil

〰〰〰〰〰〰〰〰〰〰〰〰〰〰〰〰〰

Serves **4**
Preparation time: **15 minutes**
Cooking time: **25 minutes**

You could call this soup a feast of alliums. Garlic, leeks and onions don't just add wonderful flavour but also come with an abundance of health-giving properties; latest research shows that just half an onion a day can help reduce the risk of bowel cancer. Don't skimp on the garlic oil dressing; it really adds the finishing touch. If butter beans aren't your thing, try swapping them for two medium potatoes for a classic leek and potato soup with a twist.

1 tbsp extra virgin olive oil
2 onions, finely chopped
4 large leeks, thinly sliced
3 long sprigs of thyme
2 bay leaves
400g/14oz can butter beans, drained and rinsed
1 litre/35fl oz/4¼ cups good-quality vegetable stock
sea salt and freshly ground black pepper
vegetarian blue cheese of choice, crumbled, to serve (optional)

Roast garlic oil
1 head of garlic, cloves separated
2 tbsp extra virgin olive oil, plus extra for drizzling
leaves from 1 long sprig of thyme
a good squeeze of lemon juice
sea salt, to taste

Preheat the oven to 200°C/400°F/Gas 6. Place the garlic cloves on a piece of foil large enough to make a loose parcel. Drizzle over a little oil and scrunch up the foil to encase the garlic. Roast in the oven for 15–20 minutes until the cloves are tender and squishy when pressed.

Meanwhile, start making the soup. Heat the olive oil in a large heavy-based saucepan over a medium-low heat, add the onions and cook for 5 minutes until tender but not coloured. Stir in the leeks and cook for another 3 minutes.

Add the thyme sprigs, bay leaves, beans and stock and bring up to the boil. Turn the heat down slightly, part cover the pan with a lid and simmer for 15 minutes or until the leeks are tender. Remove the thyme and bay leaves and squeeze in all but 4 cloves of the roasted garlic. Use a stick/immersion blender to blend the soup until smooth and season with salt and pepper.

To make the roast garlic oil, squeeze the remaining garlic into a bowl, add the oil and mash together with a fork. Stir in the thyme and lemon juice, then season with salt.

Ladle the soup into bowls and add a drizzle of the roast garlic oil and crumble over some blue cheese, if using.

. . . .

PART-TIME VARIATION

Roast-chicken topping Roast a couple of skinless, boneless chicken thighs at the same time as the garlic. Season and lightly oil the chicken, place in a roasting pan and roast for 30–35 minutes or until cooked through with no trace of pink. Shred the chicken and arrange on top of each bowl of soup in place of the cheese, before drizzling over the garlic oil. You could also use leftover roast chicken, cut into thin slices.

Baked eggs with spring greens

≈≈≈≈≈≈≈≈≈≈≈≈≈≈≈≈≈≈≈≈≈≈≈≈≈≈≈≈≈≈≈≈≈≈≈≈≈

In this recipe, the baked eggs sit on a bed of green veg and new potatoes, rather than the more usual tomato-based version called 'shakshuka'. It also features another favourite, purple sprouting broccoli, which is at its best in spring. The dish comes with a bright citrusy burst from the lemon juice and zest, complemented by the lemony nuance of the coriander seeds. That said, it's a blank canvas when it comes to flavourings; you could try an Asian version with a little fresh root ginger, soy sauce and sesame oil instead.

Serves **4**
Preparation time: **10 minutes**
Cooking time: **14 minutes**

2 tsp coriander seeds
2 tbsp olive oil
450g/1lb cooked new potatoes in their skins, roughly chopped
300g/10½oz spring/collard greens, thinly sliced
6 spring onions/scallions, thinly sliced
150g/5oz purple sprouting broccoli or long-stem broccoli, stalks sliced diagonally
2 large garlic cloves, finely chopped
finely grated zest and juice of 1 unwaxed lemon
4 large eggs
sea salt and freshly ground black pepper

Topping
125g/4½oz/generous ½ cup Greek yogurt
2 tbsp tahini
2 tbsp toasted pumpkin seeds
chilli oil or dried chilli/hot pepper flakes

First, toast the coriander seeds in a small frying pan over a medium-low heat for about 1 minute, until they smell aromatic. Put the seeds in a pestle and grind with a mortar to a coarse powder. Set aside.

Heat half of the oil in a large, deep sauté pan (with a lid) over a medium heat and fry the potatoes for about 5 minutes or until they start to turn golden and crisp. Remove the potatoes with a slotted spoon, then add the remaining oil. When the oil is hot, stir in all the vegetables. Stir-fry for 3 minutes until softened, but still crisp. Add the garlic, coriander seeds and lemon zest, then stir-fry for another 1 minute. Season with salt and plenty of pepper, return the potatoes to the pan and squeeze in the lemon juice.

Make 4 indentations in the vegetables, evenly spaced apart, and crack an egg into each indentation. Cover with a lid and cook over a medium-low heat for 3–4 minutes, until the egg whites are set, but the yolks are still runny.

Mix together the yogurt and tahini, with a splash of warm water, if needed. Spoon the eggs and veg into 4 large shallow bowls and top with the tahini yogurt, pumpkin seeds and a drizzle of chilli oil or a scattering of dried chilli/hot pepper flakes.

. . . .

PART-TIME VARIATION

Baked eggs with greens and chorizo crumbs Replace the pumpkin seeds and chilli with 60g/2¼oz diced chorizo sausage. Cook in a large dry frying pan (you don't need to add any extra oil) for 5 minutes or until crisp. Top the baked eggs with the tahini yogurt and chorizo.

Green minestrone with wild garlic pesto

~~~~~~

Perfect if you're looking for a simple, warming meal that makes the most of plentiful amounts of fresh green vegetables, particularly if there are any lurking in the refrigerator that need using up. The wild garlic pesto adds oomph to the finished broth, but really isn't essential. Alternatively, swap for chives, thyme or rosemary (or a combination), or there's nothing wrong with a good-quality shop-bought pesto.

Serves **4**
Preparation time: **20 minutes**
Cooking time: **25 minutes**

75g/2½oz/¾ cup shelled broad/
    fava beans, fresh or frozen
2 tbsp extra virgin olive oil
1 large onion, finely sliced
1.2 litres/40fl oz/5 cups good-
    quality hot vegetable stock
2 tbsp tomato purée/paste
1 tbsp fresh thyme leaves or 1 tsp
    dried
1 sprig fresh rosemary, kept whole
    (optional)
2 large bay leaves
125g/4½oz orzo pasta or new
    potatoes, cubed
2 leeks, thinly sliced
150g/5½oz spring/collard greens,
    thinly sliced
squeeze of lemon juice
sea salt and freshly ground black
    pepper

Wild garlic pesto
2 good handfuls of wild garlic
    leaves, roughly sliced
1 handful blanched almonds
100ml/3½fl oz/scant ½ cup extra
    virgin olive oil, plus extra for
    drizzling
1 handful of finely grated
    vegetarian parmesan

To make the pesto, put the wild garlic leaves and almonds in a mini food processor (or use a hand-held/immersion blender and beaker) and process until finely chopped. Add the oil in two batches and continue to blend to make a coarse paste. Stir in the parmesan and season to taste. Spoon the pesto into a bowl and drizzle over a little extra olive oil, which will help to preserve the pesto and keep its colour. Set aside (it will keep in the refrigerator for up to 2 days).

Steam the broad/fava beans for 3 minutes until tender, then refresh under cold running water. Pop the beans out of their grey outer shells and set aside the bright green beans.

Meanwhile, heat the oil in a large saucepan over a medium-low heat, add the onion and cook for 7 minutes, covered, until softened but not coloured. Pour in the stock, then stir in the tomato purée/paste and herbs. Bring to the boil, then add the orzo or potatoes and cook for 7 minutes, stirring occasionally to make sure the pasta doesn't stick to the bottom of the pan.

Add the leeks and spring/collard greens, stir, and cook for another 5 minutes or until the orzo or potatoes and vegetables are tender, adding the beans in the last minute to warm through. Add a splash more stock, if needed. Remove the bay leaves and rosemary sprig. Add a squeeze of lemon and season with salt and pepper. Serve in large bowls with a spoonful of pesto and a drizzle of olive oil.

· ·
PART-TIME VARIATIONS

Green minestrone with dairy-free pesto For a vegan version of the wild garlic pesto, omit the parmesan and add 3 tbsp nutritional yeast flakes and 1 tbsp lemon juice.

Chicken and vegetable minestrone Halve the quantity of leeks and replace with 115g/4oz shredded cooked chicken. Replace the vegetable stock with chicken stock.

Broad bean humous
with artichokes and pitta crisps

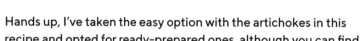

Hands up, I've taken the easy option with the artichokes in this recipe and opted for ready-prepared ones, although you can find fresh new-season artichokes in late spring. Homemade humous is a snitch to make and this one is flavoured – and coloured – with seasonal broad/fava beans. It makes a great base for the smoked paprika artichokes.

Serves **4**
Preparation time: **20 minutes**
Cooking time: **13 minutes**

300g/10½oz/2¾ cups cooked broad/fava beans
4 pitta breads
400g/14oz can chickpeas/garbanzo beans, drained, reserving 4 tbsp liquid from the can
4 garlic cloves, peeled
juice of 2 lemons, or more to taste
4 tbsp tahini
6 tbsp extra virgin olive oil, plus extra for drizzling
300g/10½oz prepared cooked artichoke hearts
1 tsp hot smoked paprika, plus extra for sprinkling
1 handful of toasted pine nuts
2 tbsp chopped fresh mint leaves
sea salt and freshly ground black pepper

Preheat the oven to 180°C/350°F/Gas 4. Remove and discard the grey outer shell of the cooked broad/fava beans and set the bright green beans aside.

Slice the pitta breads along the long edge and open out into two halves, then cut them down the middle to separate the halves. Place them straight onto the oven shelves and bake for 10 minutes or until crisp and slightly golden. Transfer to a wire cooling rack and drizzle over a little olive oil and a dusting of paprika. Set aside to cool.

Meanwhile, make the humous. Put the chickpeas and 2 of the garlic cloves in a food processor or blender and pulse until almost smooth. Add two-thirds of the broad/fava beans, the juice of 1½ lemons, the tahini and 4 tablespoons of the olive oil. Pulse until smooth and creamy, season with salt and pepper, then pulse again. Taste and add more seasoning or lemon juice, if needed. Set aside.

To prepare the artichokes, heat the remaining 2 tablespoons of olive oil in a large frying pan over a medium-low heat. Add the artichokes and the remaining garlic. Cook for 2 minutes, stirring, then add the paprika and juice of ½ lemon. Season and warm through, then taste and add more lemon juice, if needed. Leave to cool slightly.

Spoon the humous into serving bowls (you will have some leftover), then top with the artichokes. Serve sprinkled with the rest of the broad/fava beans, the pine nuts and mint. Serve with the pitta crisps.

. . . .

PART-TIME VARIATION

Broad bean humous with lamb Replace the artichokes with 200g/7oz lean minced/ground lamb. Heat 2 tsp olive oil in a large frying pan over a medium heat. Add the lamb and cook, breaking it up, for 10 minutes until browned. Add 2 crushed garlic cloves and cook for 1 minute, then add 1 tsp smoked paprika. Season. To serve, spoon the lamb on top of the humous and add the rest of the broad beans, pine nuts and mint. Serve with the pitta bread crisps.

Tomato bulgur
with raw asparagus salad and mint yogurt

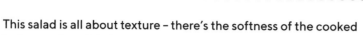

This salad is all about texture – there's the softness of the cooked bulgur grains with the crunchy, freshness of the raw asparagus and sugar snap topping, and then the smooth, creaminess of the citrusy mint yogurt.

Serves **4**
Preparation time: **15 minutes**
Cooking time: **15–18 minutes**,
plus 5 minutes standing

250g/9oz/1½ cups bulgur wheat, rinsed

1½ tbsp tomato purée/paste

1 heaped tsp vegetable bouillon powder

8 asparagus spears, woody ends trimmed, halved crossways and cut into long, thin slivers

2 large handfuls of sugar snap peas, cut in half lengthways

4 spring onions/scallions, shredded

juice of 1 lemon

1½ tbsp extra virgin olive oil, plus extra for drizzling

125ml/4½fl oz/generous ½ cup plain Greek-style yogurt, or dairy-free alternative

1 handful of fresh mint leaves, finely chopped

sea salt and freshly ground black pepper

Put the bulgur wheat in a pan along with 600ml/21fl oz/2½ cups water and bring to the boil. Stir in the tomato purée/paste and bouillon powder, then reduce the heat to its lowest setting, cover, and simmer for 12–15 minutes, or until the grains are tender but not mushy. Leave to stand for 5 minutes.

While the bulgur is cooking, put the asparagus, sugar snaps and spring onions/scallions in a bowl and add half the lemon juice and the olive oil. Season with salt and pepper and gently mix until combined.

To make the mint yogurt, spoon the yogurt into a bowl and stir in the remaining lemon juice and mint, then season to taste.

When the bulgur is ready, add a splash of olive oil and turn with a fork to fluff up the grains. Tip it into a serving bowl and top with the salad. Serve with a spoonful of the yogurt.

PART-TIME VARIATIONS

Topping ideas This salad lends itself to a variety of toppings: try a poached egg and toasted pumpkin seeds; crumbled soft goat's cheese or other crumbly cheese; a mixture of toasted walnuts and sunflower seeds; a pan-fried mackerel fillet; or slices of Parma ham, crisped up in a dry frying pan.

Black bean noodles
with purple sprouting broccoli

Spring is the season for purple sprouting broccoli with its long, elegant stem crowned with a floret of purple flowers. It's best cooked briefly to ensure it still has some crunch, so stir-frying is perfect. Some supermarkets sell packages or jars of preserved black beans, but they can readily be found in Asian food shops. These tiny beans are quite salty, so they need soaking before use, but they are worth it for the intense burst of flavour they give.

Serves **4**
Preparation time: **15 minutes**, plus **20 minutes soaking**
Cooking time: **10 minutes**

60g/2¼oz/6 tbsp Chinese salted black beans (fermented/preserved black beans)
225g/8oz firm smoked tofu, drained and patted dry
2 tbsp dark soy sauce
2 tbsp sunflower oil
4 nests of medium egg noodles, about 250g/9oz total weight
125g/4½oz purple sprouting broccoli or long-stem broccoli, woody ends trimmed
3 large garlic cloves, finely chopped
1 thumb-sized piece of fresh root ginger, peeled and finely grated
1 serrano red chilli, seeds left in, finely chopped
100g/3½oz curly kale, tough stems removed
1½ tbsp cornflour/cornstarch, stirred into 1 tbsp water
2 tsp runny honey
1 tbsp sesame oil
1 tbsp toasted sesame seeds
sea salt and freshly ground black pepper

Soak the black beans in 200ml/7fl oz/scant 1 cup warm water for 20 minutes, until softened, then drain and reserve the soaking water. At the same time, marinate the tofu in 1 tablespoon of the soy sauce.

Heat 1 tablespoon of the oil in a large wok or frying pan over a high heat, add the tofu and soy sauce marinade and fry for 5 minutes, turning occasionally, or until golden all over. Remove from the pan with a slotted spoon and set aside.

Meanwhile, cook the noodles following the package directions, adding the broccoli 1 minute before the end of the cooking time. Drain, return to the pan and cover with cold water.

Turn the heat to medium, then add the remaining 1 tablespoon of oil to the wok or pan, followed by the garlic, ginger, chilli and kale. Add the black beans and stir-fry for 2 minutes.

Add the reserved bean soaking water, cornflour/cornstarch mixture, honey, sesame oil and the remaining 1 tablespoon of soy sauce and stir-fry for another 2 minutes. Using tongs, scoop the still-wet noodles and broccoli out of the pan and add to the bean mixture along with the tofu and warm through briefly, tossing until everything is combined. Taste and season with salt and pepper, if needed, then serve sprinkled with sesame seeds.

· ·

PART-TIME VARIATION

Black bean and beef noodles Black beans and beef are a classic Chinese union. Replace the tofu with 225g/8oz lean steak, cut into thin strips for stir-frying. Marinade in 1 tbsp dark soy sauce for 15 minutes. Heat 1 tbsp sunflower oil in a large wok or frying pan over a high heat, add the beef and marinade and stir-fry for 2 minutes, turning occasionally, or until just cooked. Remove from the pan with a slotted spoon and set aside. Return to the wok to briefly warm through just before serving.

Watercress, pink grapefruit and quinoa salad

Watercress is at its best at this time of year and lends a peppery vibrancy to this immune system-boosting salad. You can also still find a good selection of citrus fruit. I've opted for pink grapefruit for its lively, refreshing taste and vibrant colour, although blood oranges, clementines or naval oranges would be equally good. The salad is substantial enough to make a light lunch or dinner, but you could also top it with toasted nuts, feta or mozzarella for a protein boost.

Serves **4**
Preparation time: **15 minutes**
Cooking time: **15 minutes**

125g/4½oz/¾ cup mixed colour quinoa, rinsed
50g/1¾oz/6 tbsp pumpkin seeds
1 pink grapefruit
100g/3½oz watercress, torn into sprigs
flesh of 2 avocados, cut into chunks
2 handfuls of alfalfa sprouts
1 large handful of fresh mint leaves, torn

Dressing
juice of 1 lemon
2 tbsp extra virgin olive oil
sea salt and freshly ground black pepper

Put the quinoa into a small saucepan with enough water to cover by 1cm/½in and bring to the boil. Reduce the heat slightly, cover with a lid, and simmer for 12–15 minutes or until it is tender but retains a little bite. Drain, refresh under cold running water and leave to cool.

Meanwhile, toast the pumpkin seeds in a large, dry frying pan over a medium-low heat for 2–3 minutes, tossing occasionally, until they start to colour – take care as they can pop out of the pan! Tip onto a plate and leave to cool.

To prepare the grapefruit, place it on a plate and cut off the top and bottom of the fruit so it can stand up. Slice off the skin and white pith, then cut into segments along the inside of the membranes that separate each one. Prise out the segments and place in a bowl. Squeeze the juice from the leftover membrane onto the plate – you should have about 4–5 tablespoons. Pour the juice into a small bowl and add the other dressing ingredients, season with salt and pepper, then mix until combined. Set aside.

Put the quinoa, watercress, grapefruit, avocados and alfalfa on a serving platter and turn gently until combined. Pour the dressing over and turn again. Taste and adjust the seasoning, if needed. Scatter over the mint and pumpkin seeds just before serving.

Red onion tarte tatin with pine nuts

≈≈≈≈≈≈≈≈≈≈≈≈≈≈≈≈≈≈≈≈≈≈≈≈≈≈≈≈≈≈≈≈

It's now easy to buy good-quality, ready-made all-butter puff pastry, so there is no need to go to the bother of making it. This savoury onion version of the classic apple-topped tarte tatin is every bit as good and makes use of new season red onions. Toasted pine nuts are sprinkled over at the end to add protein, while crumbled soft goat's cheese or feta, or toasted pumpkin seeds, would make equally tasty toppings.

Serves **4**
Preparation time: **20 minutes**
Cooking time: **35–40 minutes,**
plus 5 minutes standing

3 red onions, peeled
55g/2oz/3½ tbsp unsalted butter
　　or dairy-free spread
1 tbsp light soft brown sugar
1 tbsp sherry vinegar
2 tsp fresh thyme leaves, plus a
　　few extra sprigs, to serve
250g/9oz ready-rolled all-
　　butter puff pastry or vegan
　　alternative
2 tbsp pine nuts, toasted
　　(optional)
sea salt and freshly ground black
　　pepper
mixed leaf salad, to serve

Preheat the oven to 200°C/400°F/Gas 6.

Slice each onion in half and then slice each half into 4 wedges, cutting them from root to stem and leaving the root intact so the wedges hold together.

Melt the butter in a 24cm/9½in frying pan, add the onion wedges and cook for 5 minutes on each side until starting to colour and soften. Carefully scoop the onions out of the pan with a slotted spoon and set aside. Add the sugar and vinegar to the pan and cook for a couple of minutes, stirring, until the mixture caramelizes. Remove the pan from the heat and place on a heatproof surface.

Neatly arrange the onion wedges in a circular pattern in the pan, remembering the tart is turned out so the onion will be on the top. Season well with salt and pepper and scatter the thyme leaves over the top.

Cut the pastry into a round, about 1.5cm/⅝in larger than the pan. Lift the pastry over the onions and tuck it in around the onions and down the side of the pan. Make 2 small slits in the top of the pastry to let the steam out. Bake for 25–30 minutes until the pastry is risen and golden. Leave to stand for 5 minutes, then cover the pan with a plate and invert the tarte onto it. Alternatively, be brave and quickly turn the tart out onto a wooden board. Scatter over the pine nuts, if using, and top with a few sprigs of thyme. Serve warm, cut into wedges, with a mixed leaf salad.

Roti with spinach saag and paneer

~~~~~~

There's something reassuringly comforting about this favourite classic of creamy spinach sauce and paneer, the mild-tasting Indian cheese. I don't fry the paneer before adding it to the spinach, but this is always an option if you prefer your paneer golden with a slight crust. You could try this dish with cubes of halloumi instead, or ditch the cheese altogether as the sauce is perfectly delicious on its own. If time is short, serve the spinach with basmati rice instead of the roti – although I do love roti and the dough can be made ahead and frozen until needed.

Serves **4**
Preparation time: **35 minutes**, plus 15 minutes resting
Cooking time: **25 minutes**

Roti
150g/5½oz/generous 1 cup plain/all-purpose flour, plus extra for dusting
½ teaspoon baking powder
large pinch of sea salt
1 tbsp melted butter or oil, for brushing

Spinach saag
small knob of butter, for frying
4 garlic cloves, finely chopped
2.5cm/1in piece of fresh root ginger, peeled and finely grated
500g/1lb 2oz spinach, tough stalks removed
250ml/9fl oz/1 cup good-quality hot vegetable stock
1 green serrano chilli, seeds left in, diced
½ tsp ground turmeric
6 tbsp double/heavy cream
good squeeze of lemon juice
250g/9oz paneer, patted dry and cut into bite-size pieces
salt and freshly ground black pepper

To make the roti, sift together the flour, baking powder and salt in a large mixing bowl and make a well in the middle. Pour 100ml/3½fl oz/scant ½ cup lukewarm water into the dry ingredients. Mix with a fork and then with your hands to form a ball of dough, adding a splash more water, if needed. Turn the dough out onto a lightly floured work surface and knead for 5 minutes to a smooth ball. Place in a clean bowl, cover and leave to rest for 15 minutes.

Divide the dough into 4 portions and roll each into a ball. Take one of the balls (keep the others covered) and roll it out to a thin round, about 18cm/7in in diameter. Brush the top with melted butter or oil and roll up into a cylinder. Turn the cylinder so it is facing lengthways towards you and roll it up again. Flatten the dough with the palm of your hand and roll it out once more into a 18cm/7in round.

Heat a large frying pan over a high heat, place the roti in the pan and cook for 2 minutes on each side until flaky and golden. Wrap the roti in foil and keep warm in a low oven while you make the rest.

Next, make the spinach saag. Melt the butter in a large deep sauté pan over a medium-low heat. Add the garlic and ginger and cook for 1 minute before adding the spinach – you may need to do this in 2 batches and wait until the first batch of spinach has wilted down a little before adding the remaining spinach. Pour in the hot stock and cook the spinach, turning it with tongs so it cooks evenly, for a couple of minutes, until wilted.

Transfer the spinach to a blender with the chilli, turmeric and cream and briefly process until roughly chopped. Return to the pan to reheat, adding a squeeze of lemon juice and the paneer, then season to taste. Warm through briefly, turning until everything is combined. Serve the spinach saag with the roti on the side.

PART-TIME VARIATIONS

Dairy-free spinach saag with tofu For a non-dairy alternative, use coconut oil instead of the butter in the roti and a vegan cream alternative in the spinach saag. Tofu (or tempeh), fried until crisp and golden, is a good alternative to the paneer.

Prawn roti Instead of the spinach saag, opt for a non-cooked topping for the roti. A heap of cooked prawns/shrimp, chives, chopped chilli, avocado, rocket/arugula leaves and sriracha sauce tastes delicious.

Topping ideas Other topping ideas include a poached or fried egg; roasted vegetables; grated raw root vegetables; kimchi; cottage cheese; leftover roasted meats or fresh white crabmeat.

Spring lunch with friends

MENU
Serves 4–6

°°

Green gazpacho

°°

Spring green and leek filo pie

°°

New-season potato and watercress salad

A celebration of spring produce: new potatoes, leeks, broad/
fava beans, spring onions/scallions, herbs, spring/collard greens,
watercress and radishes. There's a beauty of a pie, which makes
a stunning centrepiece to a meal. The pie comes with a herby
watercress and potato salad – Jersey Royals are a favourite, but
any new season waxy potato would be good. It's best to pour the
vinaigrette dressing over the potatoes while they're still warm to
allow it to seep in, rather than sit on the surface, before adding the
rest of the salad ingredients. Serve it at room temperature, rather
than refrigerator cold. To save time on the day, make the gazpacho a
day in advance; the same goes for the pie filling.

Green gazpacho

Preparation time: 15 minutes, plus overnight chilling, plus 1 hour further chilling
Cooking time: 5 minutes

75g/2½oz/generous ½ cup cashew nuts
30g/1oz fresh chives (with flowers, if available, for garnish)
100g/3½oz baby spinach leaves
75g/2½oz watercress
1 green serrano chilli, roughly chopped
1 large garlic clove, peeled
4 spring onions/scallions, trimmed
500ml/17fl oz/2 cups good-quality chilled vegetable stock
1–2 tbsp sherry vinegar
2 tbsp mild-tasting extra virgin olive oil
1 ripe avocado, halved, stone and skin removed, sliced
sea salt and freshly ground black pepper

Topping
4 tbsp plain Greek-style yogurt or dairy-free alternative
dried chilli/hot pepper flakes

Soak 55g/2oz/scant ½ cup of the cashews for at least 1 hour in warm water. When ready, drain, discarding the soaking water, then put them in a blender with the chives, spinach, watercress, chilli, garlic, spring onions/scallions and stock. Pulse until the mixture is smooth and creamy. Add 1 tablespoon of the vinegar and the olive oil, season generously with salt and pepper and blend again. Tip into an airtight container and chill overnight (or make the gazpacho in the morning to eat that evening).

When chilled, add three-quarters of the avocado and blend again until smooth and creamy. Chill for another 1 hour.

When chilled, taste and add the rest of the vinegar, adjust the seasoning and add more stock, if you feel the gazpacho needs it.

Toast the remaining cashews in a large, dry frying pan for about 5 minutes, tossing them occasionally, until golden in places. Leave to cool, then roughly chop. Serve the gazpacho in small cups or bowls, topped with a spoonful of yogurt, the remaining avocado, toasted cashews, a few dried chilli/hot pepper flakes and the chive flowers, if you have them.

. . . .
PART-TIME VARIATION

Green gazpacho with prosciutto topping Swap the toasted cashew topping for 2 slices of crispy prosciutto. Dry-fry the slices in a large frying pan until crisp. Drain on paper towels and place on top of the gazpacho with the yogurt, avocado, dried chilli/hot pepper flakes and chive flowers.

Spring green and leek filo pie

Preparation time: 20 minutes | Cooking time: 45–50 minutes

75g/2½oz/5 tbsp butter, melted
3 leeks, chopped
3 garlic cloves, finely chopped
500g/1lb 2oz spring/collard greens, tough
    stalks removed, leaves shredded
3 eggs, lightly beaten
140g/5oz mature vegetarian Cheddar
    cheese, grated
4 tbsp double/heavy cream
large pinch of freshly grated nutmeg
handful of fresh mint leaves, chopped
4 large sheets of filo pastry
sea salt and freshly ground black pepper

Heat 25g/1oz/1½ tbsp of the butter in a saucepan over a medium heat. Add the leeks, turn the heat to low and sauté for 6 minutes, stirring often, until softened but not browned. Add the garlic and cook for another 2 minutes.

Meanwhile, steam the greens for 1½ minutes until just tender – it's best to do this in 2 batches to allow the greens to cook evenly. Refresh under cold running water so they keep their colour and stop cooking. Drain well and squeeze out any excess water with your hands. Tip the greens into a mixing bowl and add the leek mixture, then leave to cool.

When cool, stir in the eggs, Cheddar, cream, nutmeg and mint, and season generously with salt and pepper.

Preheat the oven to 200°C/400°F/Gas 6. Melt the remaining butter in a small pan. Lightly brush a deep 22cm/8½in springform cake pan with some butter.

To assemble the pie, brush one of the sheets of filo with a little butter and place in the prepared pan, letting any excess pastry hang over the top. Brush a second sheet of filo with butter and place it across the first sheet. Repeat with the remaining sheets of filo, crossing them over in the pan so the base and sides are covered. Spoon in the cooled filling mixture, then fold the overhanging pastry over the filling, scrunching it as you go. It should partly cover the pastry, leaving the central part of the pie open. Brush the pastry top and filling with the rest of the melted butter.

Bake the pie for 35–40 minutes until the pastry is golden and crisp. Leave to sit in the pan for 5 minutes, then release from the pan before serving warm with the potato and watercress salad.

New-season potato and watercress salad

Preparation time: 15 minutes | Cooking time: 15 minutes

800g/1lb 12oz waxy new potatoes,
 preferably Jersey Royals, skins left
 on and scrubbed, halved or quartered
 if large
125g/4½oz/1 cup shelled broad/fava beans
 or peas, fresh or frozen
100g/3½oz radishes, thinly sliced into
 rounds
3 spring onions/scallions, finely sliced
3 large handfuls of watercress, torn into
 small sprigs
1 handful of fresh mint leaves, finely
 chopped
1 handful of fresh chives, snipped
 (including flowers, if available)

Dressing
2 tbsp extra virgin olive oil
2 tbsp apple cider vinegar
½ tsp wholegrain mustard
sea salt and freshly ground black pepper

Cook the potatoes in plenty of boiling salted water until tender, about 15 minutes. At the same time, steam the broad/fava beans or peas until tender, then refresh under cold running water. Pop the beans out of their outer casings.

Mix together the ingredients for the dressing until combined and season with salt and pepper.

Put the warm potatoes in a bowl, pour the dressing over, then turn with a spoon to coat the potatoes. Leave them to cool slightly, then fold in the beans or peas, radishes and spring onions/scallions.

Arrange the watercress on a large serving platter. Spoon the potato salad on top and serve sprinkled with the herbs and chive flowers, if available.

. . . .
PART-TIME VARIATION

New-season potato, salmon and watercress salad Swap half of the beans or peas with 1 cooked, skinless smoked salmon (or mackerel) fillet. Flake into pieces and fold the fish in at the end with the rest of the beans/peas, radishes and spring onions/scallions. Serve as above.

chargrilled asparagus with wild garlic mash

I'm very lucky to share an allotment with a group of friends, and this time of year is an absolute joy as we are rewarded with plentiful amounts of fresh asparagus. It's also the time of year for wild garlic, which grows abundantly in woodland areas, but do swap with spring onions/scallions or chives if they are more readily available to you.

Serves **4**
Preparation time: **20 minutes**
Cooking time: **30 minutes**

300g/10½oz asparagus spears, woody ends trimmed
12 spring onions/scallions, about 2 bunches, trimmed
olive oil, for brushing
splash of white wine or cider vinegar
8 eggs
sea salt and freshly ground black pepper

Wild garlic mash
900g/2lb white potatoes for mashing, peeled and quartered
40g/1½oz/2½ tbsp unsalted butter
75–100ml/2½–3½fl oz/⅓–scant ½ cup whole/full-fat milk
60g/2¼oz wild garlic leaves, or spring onions/scallions or chives, finely chopped

Mustard mayo
4 tbsp mayonnaise
4 tsp English mustard

Mix together the mustard mayo ingredients, adding 3–4 tablespoons water to make a creamy sauce consistency, season, then set aside.

For the mash, cook the potatoes in plenty of boiling salted water until tender, 10–15 minutes. Drain, then return the potatoes to the hot pan, place over a low heat and add the butter, milk and wild garlic. Turn off the heat when warmed through, then mash until smooth and creamy, adding more milk, if needed. Season.

Meanwhile, heat a griddle/grill pan over a high heat. Brush the asparagus and spring onions/scallions with oil and chargrill in 2–3 batches for 7–10 minutes each time, turning occasionally, until charred in places and tender. Keep warm in a low oven.

Finally, poach the eggs. Three-quarters fill a large deep sauté pan with water and heat to boiling point. Reduce the heat to low, add a splash of vinegar and swirl the water with a spoon. Crack one of the eggs into a cup then carefully lower it into the simmering water, and poach for 3 minutes or until the white is set but the yolk remains runny. Cook no more than 4 eggs at a time. Remove from the pan with a slotted spoon and drain on paper towels.

To serve, reheat the mash, if needed, and spoon onto plates. Top with the chargrilled veg and eggs, season with salt and pepper and serve with a spoonful of mustard mayo.

PART-TIME VARIATIONS

Trout Replace the eggs with 4 pink trout fillets. Preheat the grill/broiler to high. Place a few dots of butter on top of each fillet, season with salt and pepper, and grill/broil for 6–8 minutes, turning once, until just cooked. When making the mustard mayo, use wholegrain instead of English mustard and add a squeeze of lemon juice.

Walnuts For a vegan alternative, use a non-dairy spread and the dairy-free milk of your choice. The eggs can be replaced with 100g/3½oz toasted roughly chopped walnuts.

Spring vegetable fritto misto
with saffron mayo

This recipe idea is inspired by a meal enjoyed at a local Italian restaurant. Spring vegetables are coated in the crispiest, golden batter, which is light enough not to mask the flavour of the vegetables. If you are put off by the idea of deep-frying, steam or chargrill the veg instead for a lower-fat option, then arrange on a platter with the golden-hued saffron mayonnaise.

Serves **4**
Preparation time: **20 minutes**
Cooking time: **15 minutes**

250g/9oz asparagus spears, woody ends trimmed
12 purple sprouting or long-stem broccoli spears, trimmed
70g/2½oz samphire

Batter
70g/2½oz/½ cup plain/all-purpose flour
70g/2½oz/½ cup cornflour/cornstarch
185ml/6fl oz/¾ cup chilled sparkling water
a large pinch of sea salt

Saffron mayo
large pinch of saffron threads or ground turmeric
2 egg yolks
1 tbsp Dijon mustard
2–3 garlic cloves, crushed (depending on your love of garlic)
150ml/5fl oz/⅔ cup mild-tasting olive oil
100ml/3½fl oz/scant ½ cup sunflower oil, plus extra for deep-frying
squeeze of lemon juice
sea salt, to taste

First, make the saffron mayonnaise. Soak the saffron in 2 teaspoons just-boiled water. Using a balloon whisk or blender, mix together the egg yolks and mustard until smooth, then stir in the garlic. Slowly add both types of oil, one drop at a time and whisking/blending continuously, until the mixture is smooth and the consistency of thick mayonnaise. Whisk in the saffron and soaking water, a squeeze of lemon juice and season with salt. Chill until ready to serve.

Place all the vegetables on a plate next to where you will be frying. Line 2 large plates with paper towels and turn the oven to a low heat.

Combine the flour and cornflour/cornstarch in a large bowl, make a well in the middle and gradually whisk in the sparkling water. Season with salt. The consistency should be similar to single/light cream.

Heat enough oil to half-fill a medium heavy saucepan to 176°C/350°F (or until a cube of bread browns in 40 seconds).

Dunk the asparagus, one spear at a time, into the batter, letting any excess drain off, then carefully lower it into the hot oil. Cook 3–4 asparagus spears at a time for about 1½ minutes until crisp and golden, then remove from the pan with a slotted spoon and drain on paper towels. Keep warm in the oven. Repeat with the broccoli and then the samphire, placing a small handful into the batter and then straight into the oil so they stick together into a 'nest'.

When all the vegetables are cooked, arrange them on a serving plate and serve with a bowl of saffron mayonnaise for dipping.

· ·
PART-TIME VARIATION

'Nduja mayo Swap the saffron mayonnaise for one flavoured with the Italian spicy pork paste, 'nduja. Replace the saffron and soaking water for 2 tablespoons 'nduja paste, stirring it in at the end. (You could also use the batter to coat seafood, such as prawns/shrimp and squid rings, instead of vegetables.)

Spiced-leek flatbreads with mint raita

These yeast-free flatbreads are filled with a mixture of mashed potato, leek, halloumi and spices and come with a mint raita. The dough is yeast-free and quick to make and you could also use it as a base for pan pizzas: roll out a quarter of the dough into a thin round, place in a lightly oiled frying pan and cook for a couple of minutes until crisp. Add your favourite toppings, then grill/broil until cooked – simple.

Makes **4**
Preparation time: **25 minutes,**
plus **20 minutes resting**
Cooking time: **25 minutes**

Dough
200g/7oz/1½ cups self-raising/
    self-rising flour, plus extra for
    dusting
½ tsp baking powder
½ tsp salt
200g/7oz/scant 1 cup plain live
    yogurt
1½ tbsp extra virgin olive oil, plus
    extra for frying

Filling
1 leek, finely chopped
175g/6oz mashed potatoes
1 tsp garam masala
½ tsp nigella seeds
100g/3½oz halloumi, patted dry
    and coarsely grated
freshly ground black pepper

Mint raita
2 handfuls of chopped mint
    leaves
150g/5oz/scant ¾ cup plain live
    yogurt
1 green jalapeño chilli, diced

First, make the dough. Sift together the flour, baking powder and salt in a mixing bowl. Make a well in the middle and add the yogurt and 1 teaspoon oil. Using a fork and then your hands, combine the mixture into a soft dough. Tip the dough onto a lightly floured work surface and knead briefly to make a smooth ball. Return the dough to the cleaned bowl, cover, and leave to rest for 20 minutes.

While the dough is resting, heat the remaining oil in a frying pan over a medium heat. Add the leek and fry for 5 minutes until softened. Spoon the leek into a bowl and stir in the mashed potato, garam masala, nigella seeds and halloumi. Season with pepper only.

Mix together all the ingredients for the raita. Season and set aside.

Divide the dough into 4 pieces. Roll them out, one at a time, into a thin round, about 3mm/⅛in thick. Spoon a quarter of the filling mixture over one half of the rolled-out dough and press it out evenly with the back of the spoon, leaving a 1cm/½in wide border. Brush the border with water and fold over the dough to encase the filling. Press it flat, then fold over the edges and pinch together to seal.

Heat a frying pan over a medium heat and brush it with oil. Place a filled flatbread in the pan and cook for 2–2½ minutes on each side, standing it up to brown the edges, until golden and cooked through. Repeat with the remaining dough and filling. Serve with the raita.

. . . .
PART-TIME VARIATION

Spiced lamb flatbreads with mint raita Instead of halloumi, use 100g/3½oz lean minced/ground lamb. Fry the lamb for 5 minutes in a splash of oil over a medium heat. Add the leek and fry for another 5 minutes, until the lamb is golden and starting to crisp. Combine with the other filling ingredients as above.

Green rice and peas

A celebration of 'green' – admittedly it's a bit early in the season for fresh peas, but frozen ones are an indispensable alternative in my house and, what's more, are available all-year-round. This sort-of pilaf comes topped with a combination of feta, spring onions/scallions and fresh mint.

Serves **4**
Preparation time: **20 minutes**
Cooking time: **25 minutes**

50g/1¾oz/3½ tbsp butter
1 onion, finely chopped
3 garlic cloves, finely chopped
300g/10½oz/scant 1¾ cups basmati rice, washed
100g/3½oz/scant 1 cup frozen peas
freshly ground black pepper

Green sauce

3 spring onions/scallions, roughly chopped
75g/2½oz Little Gem/Bibb lettuce
2 green serrano chillies, seeds in
2 large handfuls of fresh mint leaves
1 tsp sea salt

To serve

2 spring onions/scallions, thinly sliced
1 green serrano chilli, deseeded and thinly sliced
feta cheese, crumbled (optional)
small handful of mint leaves

Put all the ingredients for the green sauce in a blender with 200ml/7fl oz/scant 1 cup water and blend to a purée. Top up with extra water to make 600ml/21fl oz/2½ cups, then set aside.

Melt three-quarters of the butter in a heavy-based saucepan over a medium-low heat. Add the onion and garlic and cook, covered and stirring occasionally, until softened, about 8 minutes.

Add the rice to the pan and stir to coat it in the buttery mixture. Stir in the green sauce and bring to the boil, then reduce the heat to its lowest setting, cover the pan with a lid, and cook for 15 minutes, or until the rice is tender and the liquid has been absorbed. Add the peas 5 minutes before the end of the cooking time and an extra splash of water, if needed. Turn off the heat and leave to sit on the warm hob for 5 minutes. Add the remaining butter, season with salt and pepper, to taste, and fluff up the rice with a fork.

Scatter the sliced spring onions/scallions and chilli over the rice, along with the crumbled feta (if using) and the mint leaves.

. . . .

PART-TIME VARIATION

Bacon topping Excuse the predictability of this alternative to the feta cheese, but peas and bacon are natural partners. Choose nitrite-free rashers of smoked streaky bacon and grill/broil until crisp. Drain on paper towels before arranging on top of the rice.

Sweet potato tortilla

~~~~~~

Spring marks the tail-end of the sweet potato season and what better way to mark this time of year than with this take on the classic Spanish tortilla? For an alternative, swap the sweet potatoes for the season's new potatoes – scrub, rather than peel, if thin-skinned, and cut into small chunks before frying for 10 minutes, or until tender.

Serves **4**
Preparation time: **15 minutes**
Cooking time: **30 minutes**

100ml/3½fl oz/scant ½ cup olive oil
350g/12oz sweet potatoes, peeled and cut into bite-size chunks
2 onions, thinly sliced
8 eggs, lightly beaten
1 tbsp fresh thyme leaves or 1 tsp dried
sea salt and freshly ground black pepper

Topping
100g/3½oz vegetarian mozzarella cheese, drained, patted dry and sliced into rounds
2 handfuls of watercress sprigs
Wild Garlic Pesto (see page 24) or shop-bought sun-dried tomato pesto

Heat the oil in a heavy-based frying pan, about 20cm/8in diameter with a heatproof handle, over a medium-low heat. Add the sweet potatoes and cook for 10 minutes, turning occasionally, then add the onions and cook for another 10 minutes, or until both are tender. Scoop the sweet potatoes and onions out of the oil, drain on paper towels, then place them in a mixing bowl. Add the eggs, season with the thyme, salt and pepper and turn gently until combined.

Pour all but 1 tablespoon of the oil out the pan, pour in the egg mixture, making sure everything is evenly distributed, then cook over a medium-low heat for 5–7 minutes or until the bottom is light golden and set – the top should still be slightly wobbly.

Meanwhile, preheat the grill/broiler to medium-high. Arrange the mozzarella on top of the tortilla and grill/broil for about 5 minutes or until the tortilla is just set and the mozzarella has melted. Serve the tortilla topped with sprigs of watercress and small blobs of pesto.

· ·
PART-TIME VARIATION

Crab topping For a seasonal shellfish topping, omit the mozzarella and replace with white crabmeat. Spoon the topping on at the end, along with sprigs of watercress, after the tortilla has finished cooking. Mix together 6 tbsp mayonnaise with the juice of ½ lemon, 1 small crushed garlic clove and season with salt and pepper. Serve the garlic mayonnaise in place of the pesto.

Springtime Korean rice bowl

≈≈≈≈≈≈≈≈≈≈≈≈≈≈≈≈≈≈≈≈≈≈≈≈≈≈≈≈≈≈≈≈≈≈≈≈≈≈

This popular Korean rice bowl perfectly fits the spec of the flexitarian kitchen, particularly if you're looking to feed people with a variety of dietary preferences at a single meal. The core of the dish – rice – remains the same, but the toppings can be varied depending on taste and season.

Serves **4**
Preparation time: **20 minutes**
Cooking time: **25 minutes**

350g/12oz/1¾ cups short grain brown or white rice, rinsed
sea salt

Sauce
2 tbsp gochujang paste or chilli sauce
1 tbsp rice wine vinegar
2 tsp honey or maple syrup
1 tbsp dark soy sauce
1 tbsp sesame oil

Toppings
2 tbsp sunflower oil
1½ tbsp sesame oil
400g/14oz mushrooms, sliced
2 large garlic cloves, finely chopped
1 tbsp dark soy sauce
300g/10½oz asparagus, woody ends trimmed
2 carrots, cut into matchsticks
1 turnip, cut into matchsticks
125g/4½oz baby spinach
4 eggs
2 spring onions/scallions, thinly sliced diagonally
black sesame seeds, for sprinkling
kimchi, to serve

Put the rice in a saucepan, pour over enough cold water to cover by 1cm/½in and season with salt. Bring to the boil, then reduce the heat to the lowest setting, cover and simmer until tender. If the rice is still firm, add a splash more water and cook, covered, for another few minutes. Turn off the heat and set aside until ready to serve.

While the rice is cooking, mix together the ingredients for the sauce and set aside.

To prepare the toppings, heat 1 tablespoon sunflower oil and another 1 tablespoon sesame oil in a large frying pan over a medium-high heat and fry the mushrooms for 10 minutes until any liquid has been absorbed and they start to turn golden and crisp. Reduce the heat to low, add the garlic and cook for another 1 minute. Add the soy sauce and cook briefly, tossing the mushrooms until dark and sticky. Tip into a bowl and keep warm in a low oven.

Wipe the pan clean, add the remaining ½ tablespoon sesame oil and the asparagus, rolling the spears in the pan to coat them in the oil. Cook for 5–7 minutes over a medium heat, turning occasionally, until just tender. Keep the asparagus warm in a low oven.

Wipe the pan clean and add the remaining 1 tablespoon sunflower oil. Break in the eggs and fry until set, but the yolks remain runny.

Meanwhile, steam the carrots, turnip and spinach for 2–3 minutes until just tender.

To serve, divide the rice between 4 large shallow bowls. Arrange the vegetables, keeping each type separate, on top of the rice, then place a fried egg in the middle. Scatter over the spring onions/scallions and sesame seeds, and drizzle with the sauce. Serve with kimchi.

• •

PART-TIME VARIATIONS

Topping ideas: pan-fried salmon, hake, seabass or squid; roast or stir-fried beef or pork; roast or stir-fried chicken, turkey or duck.

lemon crumbs and crispy capers

~~~~~~~~~~~~~~~~~~~~~~~~~~~~~~

this season's purple sprouting broccoli in this simple pasta dish. The lemon-infused crispy breadcrumbs add a lovely crunch, and if you have any left over, store in an airtight container for up to 3 days. If making your own breadcrumbs, use bread – preferably one with an open-textured crumb – that's a couple of days old.

Serves **4**
Preparation time: **15 minutes**
Cooking time: **20 minutes**

4 tbsp extra virgin olive oil

125g/4½oz/2 cups fresh chunky breadcrumbs, from about 3 slices of bread, or dried panko crumbs

finely grated zest and juice of 1 large unwaxed lemon

2 tsp fresh thyme leaves or 1 tsp dried

500g/1lb 2oz dried linguine pasta

3 tbsp non-pareil capers, drained and rinsed

200g/7oz purple sprouting broccoli, or long-stem broccoli, stalks sliced diagonally and florets left whole

2 garlic cloves, finely chopped

½ tsp dried chilli/hot pepper flakes

1 handful of fresh flat-leaf parsley, chopped

sea salt and freshly ground black pepper

vegetarian Parmesan, sliced into shavings, to serve (optional)

Heat 1 tablespoon of the oil in a large sauté pan over a medium heat, add the breadcrumbs and fry, stirring often, for 5–7 minutes until golden and crisp. Tip into a bowl, stir in the lemon zest and thyme and set aside to cool.

Cook the linguine in plenty of boiling salted water following the package directions. Drain the pasta, saving a cupful of the cooking water.

Meanwhile, wipe the sauté pan clean, add another tablespoon of olive oil and cook the capers until crisp and starting to colour. Remove with a slotted spoon and drain on paper towels.

Heat the remaining olive oil in the sauté pan, add the broccoli and fry for 5 minutes, turning occasionally, until slightly tender but still with a bit of crunch. Reduce the heat slightly, add the garlic and cook for another 2 minutes.

Add the pasta to the sauté pan along with the lemon juice and chilli/hot pepper flakes. Pour in 200ml/7fl oz/scant 1 cup of the cooking water, season, then toss using tongs until combined. Add more of the water, if the pasta appears dry. Spoon into 4 large shallow bowls and scatter over the crumbs, capers and parsley. Place the shaved Parmesan on the table and let everyone help themselves.

. . . .

PART-TIME VARIATIONS

Linguine with broccoli, lemon crumbs and anchovy Cook 3 drained anchovy fillets (in oil, rather than salted) along with the broccoli. They should break down and melt into the oil.

Linguine with broccoli, lemon crumbs and lardons Swap the capers for 100g/3½oz/¾ cup lardons or cubed smoked pancetta. Add to a dry frying pan and cook for 8–10 minutes or until crisp and light golden. Drain on paper towels and scatter over the linguine with the crumbs and parsley.

Dairy-free cacio e pepe

A vegan take on the hugely popular *cacio e pepe*, the classic Italian, pecorino-rich, creamy spaghetti dish. White miso and walnuts replace the cheese (you could also add a couple of tablespoons of nutritional yeast flakes for an extra 'cheesy' hit), while dried chilli/hot pepper flakes add a boost to the more usual heat of the freshly ground black pepper.

Serves **4**
Preparation time: **10 minutes**
Cooking time: **15 minutes**

400g/14oz dried spaghetti
125g/4½oz/scant 1 cup walnut halves
4 tbsp olive oil
4 garlic cloves, finely chopped
4 tbsp white miso
½ tsp dried chilli/hot pepper flakes
sea salt and freshly ground black pepper
2 large handfuls of rocket/arugula leaves, to serve

Cook the spaghetti in plenty of salted boiling water following the package directions.

While the pasta is cooking, toast the walnuts in a large, dry frying pan for 5 minutes, turning halfway, until they start to colour and smell toasted – watch them as they can burn in the blink of an eye.

Heat the olive oil in a large frying pan and sauté the garlic for 1 minute. Pour the garlic oil into a small blender and add the toasted walnuts (saving 8 to scatter over at the end), the miso, dried chilli/hot pepper flakes and 4 tablespoons water, then blend to a coarse paste. Roughly chop the reserved walnuts.

Drain the pasta, reserving 200ml/7fl oz/scant 1 cup of the cooking water. Return the pasta to the pan, add the sauce and enough water to make a creamy sauce – you will probably need most of it. Using tongs, turn the pasta until it is coated in the sauce and reheat it briefly if you feel you need to. Taste for seasoning and add more salt, pepper and chilli flakes, if needed. Spoon into 4 large, shallow bowls and top with a handful of rocket/arugula leaves and the reserved walnuts.

Harissa-roasted new potatoes
with beans and halloumi

No faff, just a roasting pan and an oven is needed to make this dish. For me, it contains everything I'm looking for in a meal: it's easy to make and a balanced combination of protein, carbs, good fats and lots of veg – and it uses new-season potatoes, too!

Serves **4**
Preparation time: **15 minutes**
Cooking time: **40 minutes**

2 tbsp harissa paste
4 tbsp extra virgin olive oil
700g/1lb 9oz new potatoes, scrubbed, skins left on
3 red onions, peeled and root ends trimmed, each cut into 6 wedges
16 vine cherry tomatoes, left whole
125g/4½oz canned butter/lima beans, drained
225g/8oz halloumi, drained and cut into bite-size cubes
sea salt and freshly ground black pepper

To serve
1 red jalapeño chilli, deseeded and thinly sliced
1 handful of fresh coriander/ cilantro leaves
Mint Raita (see page 46)

Preheat the oven to 200°C/400°F/Gas 6.

Mix together three-quarters of the harissa paste and olive oil in a large mixing bowl, then season with salt and pepper. Add the potatoes and onions and turn to coat them in the mixture, then tip them into a large roasting pan. Roast for 20 minutes.

Mix together the rest of the harissa paste and olive oil in the bowl, then season. Add the tomatoes and butter/lima beans and turn to coat them in the mixture, then tip into the roasting pan with the potatoes and onions and turn until combined; you may need to divide everything between 2 pans if it looks too crowded. Scatter over the halloumi and return the pan(s) to the oven for a further 20 minutes.

Serve the roasted vegetables, beans and halloumi topped with the chilli, coriander/cilantro and a good spoonful of the mint raita.

· ·

PART-TIME VARIATION

Harissa-roasted new potatoes with beans and white fish Replace the halloumi with 4 thick fillets white fish (sustainably sourced). Wrap them in individual foil parcels with a slice of lemon or lime and sliced cherry tomatoes. Drizzle over a little olive oil and season with salt and pepper. Place on a baking sheet and roast in the oven at the same time as the potatoes, for 15–18 minutes, or until opaque and flaky.

Spanish-style baked beans with almond aioli

〜〜〜〜〜〜〜〜〜〜〜〜〜〜〜〜〜〜〜〜〜〜〜〜〜〜〜〜〜

A great throw-together supper dish, this is made largely with storecupboard ingredients and makes a perfect weekday meal. The almond aioli can be made in advance and will happily sit in the refrigerator for up to 3 days. I know it's a tad early for tomatoes but by late spring they are around.

Serves **4**
Preparation time: **15 minutes,**
plus 1 hour soaking
Cooking time: **35 minutes**

2 tbsp extra virgin olive oil, plus extra for drizzling
2 onions, finely chopped
3 garlic cloves, finely chopped
300ml/10½fl oz/1¼ cups good-quality vegetable stock
3 tbsp tomato purée/paste
2 tsp dried oregano
2 tsp hot smoked paprika
2 x 400g/14oz cans cannellini beans, drained
4 vine tomatoes, sliced into rounds
100g/3½oz day-old fresh breadcrumbs
40g/1½oz vegetarian manchego or mature Cheddar cheese, coarsely grated (optional)
sea salt and freshly ground black pepper
crisp green salad, to serve

Almond aioli
150g/5½oz blanched almonds
2 tbsp extra virgin olive oil
2 garlic cloves, peeled
2 heaped tsp Dijon mustard
150ml/5½fl oz/⅔ cup almond milk or water
juice of 1 small lemon

First, start to prepare the almond aioli. Toast the almonds in a large dry frying pan over a medium-low heat for about 5 minutes, turning halfway, or until starting to colour. Tip them into a bowl, cover with water and leave to soak for 1 hour.

Just before you start to prepare the beans, preheat the oven to 180°C/350°F/Gas 4.

Heat the oil in a large frying pan over a medium heat, add the onions and fry for 7 minutes until softened. Stir in the garlic and cook, stirring, for another 2 minutes before adding the stock, tomato purée/paste, oregano, smoked paprika and beans. Season with salt and pepper and mix until combined, then transfer to a baking dish.

Arrange the tomatoes on top of the bean mixture in an even layer and scatter over the breadcrumbs and cheese, if using. Drizzle a little extra oil over the top and bake for 25 minutes or until the top is crisp.

While the beans are baking, finish making the aioli. Drain the almonds and put them in a mini food processor or blender with the oil, garlic, mustard, almond milk or water and lemon juice and blend until smooth and creamy. Season with salt and pepper and add more lemon juice or milk/water if needed – it should be the same consistency as mayonnaise.

Serve the baked beans with a good spoonful of aioli and a crisp green salad on the side.

· ·

PART-TIME VARIATION

Spanish-style baked beans with chorizo In keeping with the Spanish theme, you could mix 75g/2½oz diced cooked chorizo sausage into the breadcrumbs instead of the grated cheese. As the chorizo is fairly oily, there is no need to add the final drizzle of olive oil.

Pak choi, miso and smoked-tofu ramen

~~~~~~

Dried mushrooms are a true asset in the vegetarian kitchen – a handful goes a long way in the flavour stakes, and they also keep for months. They are great for adding flavour, texture and substance to broths, stocks, stir-fries and stews. White miso has a slightly more delicate taste than the darker alternatives, but you could use the latter if more convenient.

Serves **4**
Preparation time: **25 minutes**
Cooking time: **20 minutes**

55g/2oz dried shiitake mushrooms
2 banana shallots, chopped
2 garlic cloves, peeled
5cm/2in piece of fresh root ginger, peeled and roughly chopped
1 tbsp sunflower oil
2½ tbsp light soy sauce
3 tbsp white miso paste
3 spring onions/scallions, white and green parts separated, thinly sliced diagonally
1 tbsp sesame oil
225g/9oz smoked tofu, drained, patted dry and cut into bite-size pieces
4 eggs
4 pak choi/bok choy, halved or quartered, if large
250g/9oz soba noodles
freshly ground black pepper
black sesame seeds, to garnish

Pour 300ml/10½fl oz/1¼ cups just-boiled water over the shiitake in a bowl and leave to soften for 20 minutes. Drain, reserving the soaking water. Squeeze out the mushrooms and thinly slice half of them.

Put the whole softened shiitake, the shallots, garlic, ginger and 3 tablespoons water in a food processor and pulse to a smooth paste.

Heat the oil in a large saucepan over a medium-low heat and fry the paste for 5 minutes, stirring. Strain in the mushroom soaking liquid and add 1 litre/35fl oz/4¼ cups just-boiled water. Bring almost to the boil, then reduce to low and stir in 2 tablespoons of soy sauce and simmer for 5 minutes. Turn off the heat and use a hand-held stick/immersion blender to blend until smooth. Stir in the miso and the white parts of the spring onions/scallions, cover and set aside.

Heat 1 tablespoon sesame oil in a large frying pan over a medium-high heat, add the tofu and fry for 5–7 minutes, until golden. Remove from the pan with a slotted spoon and keep warm in a low oven. Add the sliced shiitake to the pan, adding a splash more oil if needed, and fry for 5 minutes. Add the remaining ½ tablespoon of soy sauce and continue to cook until the mushrooms are crisp. Set aside.

Meanwhile, hard-boil the eggs for about 6 minutes or until the whites are set and the yolks remain runny. Drain and briefly hold under cold running water to cool slightly, then peel.

Steam the pak choi/bok choy until tender, then cut in half.

To serve, reheat the broth over a low heat, taste and season with pepper and extra soy sauce, if needed. Cook the noodles following the package directions, drain and divide between 4 bowls. Spoon the hot broth over. Cut the eggs in half and place on top with the tofu, mushrooms and pak choi/bok choy. Scatter over the green parts of the spring onions/scallions and the black sesame seeds.

· ·

PART-TIME VARIATION

Pak choi, miso and chicken ramen Replace the tofu with 2 chicken breasts, cut into thin strips. Cook in the same way as the tofu.

SUMMER

Summer

The warm, light months of summer bring with them an abundance of fresh produce. It is when many vegetables (and fruits) are at their most bountiful and generous, from courgettes/zucchini and tomatoes to green beans and salad leaves. Summer is perhaps the easiest time of year to eat well, with seasonal dishes such as salads, chargrills and roasted vegetables taking minimal time to prepare and cook – if at all. It is a time to welcome fresh ingredients, full of colour and vibrancy.

Seasonal vegetables:

Aubergine/eggplant (peak)

Beetroot/beets (peak)

Broad/fava bean (peak)

Broccoli (peak)

Cabbage, green (in season)

Carrot (peak)

Cauliflower (in season)

Celery (in season)

Chard (peak)

Courgette/zucchini (peak)

Cucumber (peak)

Fennel (peak)

Garlic (peak)

Globe artichoke (peak)

Greens (peak)

Kale (in season)

Lettuce (peak)

Onion (in season)

Onion, spring/scallion (peak)

Pea (peak)

Pepper and chilli (peak)

Potato (peak)

Potato, new (peak)

Radish (peak)

Rocket/arugula (peak)

Samphire (peak)

Shallot (peak)

Spinach (peak)

Sugar snap pea (peak)

Sweetcorn (peak)

Tomato (peak)

Turnip (in season)

Watercress (peak)

Salt-cured carrot lox on rye

〰〰〰〰〰〰〰〰〰〰〰〰〰〰〰〰〰〰〰〰〰〰

Who would have thought that carrots baked in a salt crust and then marinated would bear a resemblance to smoked salmon? Liquid smoke may sound a bit 'Heston', but this dark liquid is now sold in large supermarkets and online and gives a rich smokiness. This recipe may be a labour of love, but it is worth giving it a try; what's more, it's a great way to make use of new-season carrots. Try baking celeriac/celery root, beetroot/beets, turnips or swede in a salt crust, too. The method keeps the root veg moist and cooks them gently and evenly.

Serves **4**
Preparation time: **15 minutes,**
plus 1–2 days marinating
Cooking time: **1 hour**

4 carrots, unpeeled and scrubbed
sea salt, to cover

Marinade
2 tbsp extra virgin olive oil
1 tsp liquid smoke or dark soy
    sauce
1 tsp apple cider vinegar

To serve
sliced rye bread, light or dark
cream cheese or non-dairy
    alternative
1 small red onion, thinly sliced into
    rounds
1 tbsp non-pareil capers, drained,
    rinsed and roughly chopped
small dill sprigs
freshly ground black pepper

Preheat the oven to 180°C/350°F/Gas 4.

Put a good layer of salt in a small ovenproof dish that is just large enough to accommodate the carrots. Wash the carrots and, while still wet, lay them on the bed of salt, making sure they don't touch the bottom of the dish. Pour more salt over the carrots until they are completely submerged. Bake for 1 hour, or until the carrots are tender and the salt forms a hard crust. Remove from the oven, then leave for a minute or so until cool enough to handle. Lift out the carrots, crack open the crust and brush off any residual salt.

Using the blunt edge of a kitchen knife, carefully rub off the carrot skin. Cut each carrot in half crossways, then thinly slice into wide strips and place in a shallow dish. Mix together the ingredients for the marinade and pour it over the carrots, turning them until evenly coated. Cover and leave to marinate in the refrigerator for 1–2 days until the carrots are soft and silky in texture. Turn them once or twice during marinating to stop them drying out.

To serve, lift the carrot lox out of the marinade; they're best served at room temperature. Spread cream cheese over the rye bread and top with a few slices of carrot and red onion. Sprinkle over a few capers and dill sprigs, then finish with a grinding of black pepper.

· ·
PART-TIME VARIATION

Smoked salmon lox with caper and dill sauce Smoked wild salmon or trout are, of course, obvious alternatives to the carrot. For an alternative topping try a caper and dill sauce: finely chop 1 tbsp drained and rinsed non-pareil capers and mix with 3 tbsp mayonnaise, the juice of ½ lemon, 1 tbsp chopped dill and 1 tbsp water. Season with black pepper. Serve the salmon or trout on rye bread with a spoonful of the sauce and an extra squeeze of lemon juice.

Eggs, avocado and black beans
with fresh tomato salsa

A breeze to throw together, this makes the best light lunch or quick supper dish. The fresh salsa – a version of the Mexican *pico de gallo* – makes the most of summer tomatoes and is a lively combination of summery ingredients. Look out for Greek basil, which has smaller leaves than regular basil and can be eaten whole without cutting or tearing, which can discolour large leaves.

Serves **4**
Preparation time: **15 minutes**
Cooking time: **5 minutes**

olive oil, for cooking

4 large eggs

2 ripe avocados, flesh sliced

400g/14oz can black beans, drained and rinsed

sea salt and freshly ground black pepper

hot chilli sauce and crusty bread, to serve (optional)

Fresh tomato salsa

6 vine tomatoes, deseeded and diced

7 radishes, diced

1 small red onion, diced

1 tbsp chopped jalapeño chillies from a jar, drained

juice of 1 lime

1 handful of basil leaves, preferably Greek, plus extra to serve

Combine all the ingredients for the fresh tomato salsa and season with salt and pepper, to taste. Set aside at room temperature.

Add enough oil to coat the base of a frying pan and set over a medium heat. Crack in the eggs and fry until the whites are set but the yolks are still runny.

Arrange the avocado slices on 4 serving plates, top with the beans, salsa and then the eggs. Season and add a drizzle of chilli sauce. Scatter over a few extra basil leaves and serve with crusty bread on the side.

· ·
PART-TIME VARIATIONS

Roast meat topping This dish is perfect for using up leftovers, especially roast chicken, beef or pork. Cut into strips and arrange on top of the avocado in place of the egg.

Vegan topping For an egg-free version, replace with crumbled flavoured seitan (the chorizo one is good), smoked tofu or flavoured tempeh, fried in a little oil for 5 minutes until slightly crisp.

Corn and tofu fritters
with tomato herb relish

〰〰〰〰〰〰〰〰〰〰〰〰〰〰〰〰〰〰〰

There's nothing better than sweetcorn at the peak of its seasonal best. The sweet, plump kernels should look bright and glossy when fresh – it is one vegetable that doesn't last that long after harvesting. Try to find cobs still in their green papery husks, rather than prepared and wrapped in plastic. Here, the corn is combined with soft silken tofu to make these fritters-cum-omelettes and served with a fresh tomato and herb relish.

Serves **4**
Preparation time: **15 minutes**
Cooking time: **12 minutes**

2 sweetcorn cobs, husks removed
200g/7oz silken tofu, drained and mashed
4 eggs, lightly beaten
4 spring onions/scallions, thinly sliced
sea salt and freshly ground black pepper
butter or olive oil, for frying
rocket/arugula salad, to serve

Tomato relish
6 vine tomatoes, deseeded and finely chopped
2 spring onions/scallions, finely chopped
1 medium-hot red chilli, diced
1 large handful of fresh flat-leaf parsley, finely chopped
juice of ½ lemon

Mix together all the ingredients for the relish, season with salt and pepper and set aside at room temperature.

Stand the corn cobs, one at a time, on their ends and slice off the kernels – you need about 200g/7oz/2 cups kernels. Place in a large bowl with the mashed tofu, eggs and spring onions/scallions, then season with salt and pepper.

Heat enough butter or oil to coat the base of a large frying pan over a medium heat. Spoon in 3–4 tablespoons of batter per fritter and cook – about 3 at a time – for 1½ minutes on each side until cooked and golden. Repeat to make about 12 fritters in total, adding more butter or oil to the pan when necessary. Keep the cooked fritters warm in a low oven while you use up the remaining batter. Serve the fritters with the tomato salsa and a rocket/arugula salad.

Roasted spiced tofu with corn chaat

Chaat, a crisp Indian savoury snack, adds heaps of colour, flavour and texture to this marinated tandoori-style tofu. Chaat masala is a zingy, slightly hot combination of cumin, coriander, black salt, chilli, dried mint, amchoor (mango powder) and ground ginger, although combinations can vary, and can be found in Asian supermarkets or online.

Serves **4**
Preparation time: **20 minutes**,
plus at least 1 hour marinating
Cooking time: **45 minutes**

400g/14oz block of firm tofu, drained and patted dry, cut into 1cm/½in thick slices
250g/9oz/generous 1 cup Greek-style plain yogurt
1 tbsp sunflower oil
2 tsp tomato purée/paste
juice of ½ small lemon
4 garlic cloves, crushed
½ tsp ground turmeric
2 tsp chaat masala, plus extra for sprinkling
½ tsp medium chilli powder
¾ tsp sea salt
juice of 1 lime
1 handful each of chopped fresh coriander/cilantro and mint leaves
5 large poppadoms, to serve

Corn chaat
100g/3½oz/¾ cup canned drained chickpeas/garbanzo beans, patted dry
1½ tsp sunflower oil
2 tsp chaat masala
2 sweetcorn cobs, husks removed
½ small red onion, diced
½ small cucumber, deseeded and diced
¼ tsp dried chilli/hot pepper flakes
juice of 1 lime

To make the marinade for the tofu, mix 150g/5½oz/¾ cup of the yogurt with the oil, tomato purée/paste, lemon juice, 3 of the garlic cloves, turmeric, chaat masala or garam masala, chilli powder and ¾ teaspoon of salt in a large shallow dish. Pat the tofu slices dry with a paper towel for a final time, then add them to the dish and spoon the marinade over to coat. Leave to marinate for at least 1 hour.

Preheat the oven to 200°C/400°F/Gas 6.

Toss the chickpeas/garbanzo beans in the oil and chaat masala until coated. Tip them onto a baking sheet and roast for 45 minutes, turning once or twice, until golden and crisp.

Meanwhile, line a baking sheet with baking paper and arrange the marinated tofu on it. Roast for 30 minutes, turning once and spooning over any leftover marinade in the dish, until light golden and crisp in places.

Hold the sweetcorn with tongs over the flame of a hob, turning it occasionally, until charred in places (you could also do this in a dry griddle/grill pan). Repeat with the second cob. Stand the cobs on their ends and slice off the kernels. Place the corn in a serving bowl with rest of the chaat ingredients and season with salt. Add the roasted chickpeas/garbanzo beans just before serving.

Mix the remaining yogurt and garlic with the lime juice. Season and stir in most of the coriander and mint. To serve, place the tofu on the poppadoms, top with a spoonful of the corn chaat, a spoonful of the herb yogurt and scatter over the remaining herbs and smashed poppadom shards. Add a sprinkling of chaat masala, if you like.

PART-TIME VARIATION

Roasted spiced chicken with corn chaat Cut 4 skinless, boneless chicken thighs into large bite-size chunks. Marinate in the spiced yogurt instead of the tofu, then roast for 30 minutes, turning once, until golden and cooked through. Serve as above.

Baked halloumi with red mojo sauce

≈≈≈≈≈≈≈≈≈≈≈≈≈≈≈≈≈≈≈≈≈≈≈≈≈≈≈≈≈≈≈≈

If you've ever travelled to the Canary Islands, the chances are you've come across the classic red or green pepper sauce called *mojo*. This version is slightly different to the classic red mojo in that the pepper is roasted before blending with the rest of the sauce ingredients. It tastes delicious with the baked halloumi, and you're making the most of the heat of the oven by cooking both at the same time.

Serves **4–6**
Preparation time: **15 minutes**
Cooking time: **30 minutes**

2 x 250g/9oz blocks of halloumi, patted dry
1 lemon, sliced into thin rounds
1 garlic clove, thinly sliced
1 tbsp fresh thyme leaves or 1 tsp dried
extra virgin olive oil, for drizzling
sea salt and freshly ground black pepper
green leaf salad and warmed pitta bread, to serve

Red mojo sauce
1 large red pepper, deseeded and cut into wedges
4 tbsp extra virgin olive oil, plus extra for drizzling
2 small slices white bread (about 55g/2oz total weight), crusts removed and torn into pieces
2 serrano red chillies, deseeded
2 garlic cloves
1½ tsp smoked paprika
½ tsp cumin seeds
1½–2 tbsp apple cider vinegar

Preheat the oven to 190°C/375°F/Gas 5.

Begin by making the mojo sauce: put the red pepper on an oiled baking sheet, drizzle over a little oil and season with salt and pepper. Roast for 30 minutes, turning once, until the pepper is blackened in places. Remove from the oven and place in a bowl, cover with cling film/plastic wrap and set aside for 10 minutes.

Meanwhile, place the halloumi on a sheet of foil large enough to make a parcel. Lift it onto a large baking sheet – it may fit on with the red pepper. Drizzle the halloumi with a little olive oil, top with lemon slices, garlic and thyme. Season and fold up the foil to make a loose parcel. Bake for 20 minutes or until softened.

To finish the sauce, peel off and discard the pepper skins and place the flesh in a food processor or blender. Add the remaining ingredients and pulse until smooth. Taste and add more seasoning and/or vinegar, if needed. Serve the halloumi cut into slices, with the mojo sauce, a salad and some pitta bread on the side.

· ·

PART-TIME VARIATIONS

Mackerel with red mojo sauce Serve the mojo sauce with pan-fried mackerel fillets instead of the halloumi.

Cauliflower steaks with red mojo sauce Preheat the oven to 190°C/375°F/Gas 5. Cut 1 small cauliflower into 4 x 2cm/¾in thick steaks. Brush all over with olive oil and arrange on a large baking sheet. Squeeze over lemon juice, season and roast for 20–25 minutes. Turn the cauliflower over halfway through roasting until tender and golden in places. Serve with the mojo sauce.

Smoked tofu with red mojo sauce Pat dry 2 x 250g/9oz blocks smoked tofu and halve each one horizontally through the middle. Heat 2 tbsp olive oil in a large frying pan over a medium heat and fry the tofu steaks for 4 minutes on each side or until crisp. Remove from the pan and serve with the mojo sauce spooned over.

Thai aubergines with sunflower seed raita

A ready-made Thai red curry paste is the perfect base for a quick and convenient marinade. If you have any coconut cream left over from making the marinade, use it to flavour the jasmine rice. Serve this with green veg, such as steamed pak choi/bok choy or Chinese greens.

Serves **4**
Preparation time: **10 minutes**
Cooking time: **55 minutes**

4 tbsp Thai red curry paste
4 tbsp thick coconut cream (the top of a can of coconut milk)
juice of 2 limes, plus extra to serve
5cm/2in piece of fresh root ginger, peeled and finely grated
2 tbsp sunflower oil
2 large aubergines/eggplants, halved lengthways and cut into 1cm/½in thick half-moons
sea salt and freshly ground black pepper
jasmine rice, to serve

Sunflower seed raita
75g/2½oz/½ cup sunflower seeds
1 garlic clove, crushed
juice of ½ lime
1 good handful of chopped fresh coriander/cilantro leaves, plus extra to serve

Start by making the sunflower seed raita. Toast the seeds in a large dry frying pan over a low-medium heat for 5 minutes, tossing the pan occasionally, or until they start to turn golden. Mix 55g/2oz/⅓ cup of the seeds with 150ml/5fl oz/⅔ cup water and leave to soak for 1 hour. Set the remaining seeds aside.

Meanwhile, preheat the oven to 200°C/400°F/Gas 6. Line 2 baking sheets with baking paper.

Mix together the red curry paste, coconut cream, lime juice, ginger and oil in a shallow dish large enough to fit the aubergine/eggplant. Season the marinade with salt and pepper. Add the aubergine/eggplant and stir until coated all over, then arrange the pieces in an even layer on the lined baking sheets. Roast for 45–50 minutes, turning once and swapping the sheets around in the oven, until golden and cooked through. Drizzle with extra oil if the aubergine/eggplant looks dry during roasting.

Meanwhile, finish making the raita. Tip the soaked seeds and their water into a blender with the garlic and lime juice and blend until smooth and creamy. Spoon into a bowl and stir in the chopped coriander/cilantro and season with salt and pepper, to taste.

Serve the aubergines/eggplants with jasmine rice and a good spoonful of raita on the side. Finish with a squeeze of lime and extra coriander/cilantro leaves sprinkled over.

. . . .

PART-TIME VARIATIONS

Thai roasted chicken with sunflower seed raita Coat 8 chicken thighs (or replace one of the aubergines/eggplants with 4 thighs) in the marinade and leave to marinate for 1 hour, covered, in the refrigerator. Roast for 30–35 minutes, until golden in places and cooked through.

For a yogurt-based raita, swap the sunflower seeds for 150g/5½oz/⅔ cup Greek-style plain yogurt and stir in the garlic, lime juice and coriander. Season with salt.

Watermelon, pitta and goat's cheese salad

~~~~~~

Full of the flavours and colours of summer, the success of this vibrant salad relies on the best-tasting ingredients, so make sure the watermelon is ripe and flavourful and the herbs are perky and fresh. Other seasonal fruit to try are peaches and nectarines, while griddled/grilled halloumi is good in place of the goat's cheese.

Serves **4**
Preparation time: **20 minutes**
Cooking time: **10 minutes**

2 pitta breads
½ small watermelon, chilled
1 cucumber, quartered lengthways, deseeded and diced
½ small red onion, thinly sliced
200g/7oz radishes, thinly sliced
2 large handfuls of fresh mint leaves, chopped
1 large handful of Greek basil leaves, or regular basil
150g/5½oz soft goat's cheese, crumbled, or dairy-free alternative
¼ tsp sumac (optional)

Dressing
3 tbsp extra virgin olive oil
finely grated zest and juice of 2 unwaxed lemons
sea salt and freshly ground black pepper

Preheat the oven to 180°C/350°F/Gas 4.

To open the pitta breads, slice them lengthways along the long edge and prise open, then cut each one into 2 halves. Place straight on the oven shelves and bake for 10 minutes or until crisp and slightly golden. Leave to cool, then break into large bite-size pieces.

Meanwhile, whisk together all the ingredients for the dressing. Season with salt and pepper, to taste, and set aside.

To prepare the watermelon, slice the fruit away from the skin (the skin can be saved to make a watermelon pickle), remove any seeds and cut into bite-size chunks. Arrange the watermelon, cucumber, onion and radishes on a serving plate. Spoon over as much dressing as you like and finish with the herbs, pitta crisps, goat's cheese and a sprinkling of sumac, if using.

· ·
PART-TIME VARIATIONS

Watermelon, pitta and spiced-nut salad Toss 2 good handfuls of almonds in olive oil that has been seasoned with smoked paprika, salt and pepper. Preheat the oven to 170°C/325°F/Gas 3. Roast the almonds for 15 minutes, turning once, or until starting to colour and smell toasted. Scatter over the salad in place of the goat's cheese.

Watermelon, pitta and seafood salad Toss 300g/10½oz raw shelled king prawns/jumbo shrimp in olive oil, seasoned with smoked paprika, salt and pepper. Cook in a large frying pan for 2–3 minutes, turning once, or until cooked through and uniformly pink. Arrange on top of the salad in place of the goat's cheese.

Watermelon, pitta and chicken salad Using the end of a rolling pin, flatten 2 chicken breasts between 2 sheets of cling film/plastic wrap until about 2cm/¾in thick. Brush the chicken with olive oil, seasoned with smoked paprika, salt and pepper. Heat a griddle/grill pan over a high heat and chargrill the chicken for 5 minutes, turning once, until cooked through and there is no sign of any pink. Slice into long strips and arrange on top of the salad in place of the goat's cheese.

Summer picnic platter

MENU

Serves 4

○ ○

Gado gado summer platter

○ ○

Wonton chips

○ ○

Mango, carrot and cardamom lassi

The beauty of this summer picnic is that it takes minimal time or effort to prepare and is perfect for sharing with vegetarians, vegans and flexitarians. I suppose it could be described as a deconstructed gado gado – the classic Indonesian salad with a peanut dressing – but maybe that sounds a bit pretentious! At its heart is an Asian peanut dip, which comes with a selection of seasonal veg and other extras for dunking. And then there are the wonton chips, which I like to call the vegetarian version of the prawn cracker/shrimp chip! Feel free to swap the accompaniments depending on favourites and what you have to hand – and that includes the flexitarian options. To complement the Asian theme, there's also a cooling creamy lassi. A perfect accompaniment to the gado gado platter, the lassi should be made just before serving or packing the picnic. Keep it in a cool container and serve with ice, if possible.

Gado gado summer platter

Preparation time: 5 minutes, plus choice of accompaniments

Peanut dip

200g/7oz/scant 1 cup good-quality smooth
   or crunchy whole peanut butter
juice of 2 limes
2 tbsp light soy sauce
1 tbsp sesame oil
1 tsp dried chilli/hot pepper flakes
5cm/2½in piece of fresh root ginger, peeled
   and minced
2 garlic cloves, minced
1 tbsp soft light brown sugar

To serve

pick your favourite accompaniments from
   the following:
cooked new potatoes
cooked green beans
hard-boiled eggs
smoked tofu, cut into fingers
cucumber, quartered lengthways, deseeded
   and cut into batons
carrots, cut into batons
radishes, trimmed
sugar snap peas
lime wedges, for squeezing
Wonton Chips (see page 78)

In a food processor, blend together all the ingredients for the peanut dip with 6 tablespoons hot water until smooth. Add more water, if needed, to make a dipping consistency.

Transfer the dip to a bowl or an airtight container with a lid. It will keep for up to 3 days in the refrigerator.

Prepare the rest of your chosen accompaniments, then arrange on a large serving platter with the peanut dip and wonton chips (see page 78) – or pack into individual containers.

. . . .

PART-TIME VARIATIONS

To serve Try prawn crackers/shrimp chips; cooked chicken, pork or beef, cut into strips; or cooked shell-on large prawns/jumbo shrimp.

Wonton chips

Preparation time: 5 minutes | Cooking time: 7 minutes

12 wonton wrappers for frying, defrosted if
   frozen
sunflower oil, for brushing
½ tsp chilli powder
sea salt, to taste

Preheat the oven to 180°C/350°F/Gas 4 and line a baking sheet with baking paper. Lightly brush both sides of each wonton wrapper with oil and place on the lined baking sheet.

Sprinkle the chilli powder over the top and bake for 5–7 minutes until light golden and crisp. Remove from the heat, sprinkle with salt and leave to cool on a wire rack while you make the peanut dip.

· ·
PART-TIME VARIATIONS

Alternative seasonings The wonton chips are dusted with chilli powder but you could try other flavourings, such as bacon salt, garlic salt, Japanese gomashio (a seasoning mix of sea salt and hulled sesame seeds), smoked paprika, togarashi or five spice.

Mango, carrot and cardamom lassi

Preparation time: 10 minutes

2 large ripe mangoes, peeled, stone
    removed, roughly chopped
1 carrot, peeled and sliced
450g/1lb/generous 2 cups Greek-style
    plain yogurt
seeds from 3 cardamom pods, ground
1 tbsp runny honey
400ml/14fl oz/1⅔ cups coconut water
juice of 1 lime
ice cubes, to serve
ground cinnamon, for sprinkling

Put the mangoes in a blender with the carrot, yogurt, ground cardamom seeds, honey, coconut water and lime juice, then blend until smooth and creamy. Transfer to a flask, or other airtight container that you can keep cool, to transport to your picnic.

To serve, place a few ice cubes in 4–6 glasses, pour in the lassi and sprinkle over a little cinnamon.

. . . .
PART-TIME VARIATION

Dairy-free mango, carrot and cardamom lassi For a dairy-free alternative, blend the mango and carrot with 400ml/14fl oz/1⅔ cups coconut milk from a carton, 450g/1lb/ generous 2 cups dairy-free yogurt of choice, seeds from 3 cardamom pods, ground, 1 tbsp maple syrup or other sweetener and the juice of 1 lime. Serve with ice and sprinkled with a little ground cinnamon.

Seaweed salad with pickled ginger

≈≈≈≈≈≈≈≈≈≈≈≈≈≈≈≈≈≈≈≈≈≈≈≈≈≈≈≈

I always like recipes that make a complete meal, so you don't have to consider what to serve them with. This sea vegetable salad is equally good served as a light meal as it is topped with the Japanese-style omelette (see page 82) for something a bit more substantial. Bags of dried sea vegetables are readily available in larger supermarkets and in Asian grocers – you'll be amazed by how far a small amount goes when it is rehydrated.

Serves **4**
Preparation time: **20 minutes**, plus 1 hour pickling
Cooking time: **20 minutes**

300g/10½oz/1½ cups short-grain brown (or white) rice
15g/½oz dried mixed sea vegetables or wakame seaweed
6 spring onions/scallions, thinly sliced diagonally
½ cucumber, quartered lengthways, deseeded and diced
8 radishes, thinly sliced
1 tbsp black sesame seeds, plus extra for sprinkling
2 tbsp sesame oil
sea salt and freshly ground black pepper

Pickled ginger
3 tbsp rice vinegar
2 tbsp caster/superfine sugar
2.5cm/1in piece of fresh root ginger, peeled and cut into very fine matchsticks

To serve
Japanese-style Omelette (see page 82), optional

First, make the pickled ginger. Mix together 2 tablespoons of the rice vinegar with the sugar in a small bowl and add the ginger. Stir until combined, then set aside for 1 hour or until ready to serve.

To make the salad, put the rice in a saucepan and pour over enough cold water to cover by 1cm/½in. Add ½ teaspoon salt and bring to the boil, then turn the heat down to the lowest setting, cover with a lid and simmer until the rice is tender and the water has been absorbed, about 15–20 minutes (white rice will take about 5 fewer minutes to cook). Leave to sit in the pan for 10 minutes.

Meanwhile, put the dried sea vegetables in a bowl and just cover with cold water. Stir and leave for 5 minutes, until rehydrated.

To finish the salad, put the warm rice in a large serving bowl with the spring onions/scallions, cucumber, radishes and black sesame seeds. Drain the sea vegetables and pickled ginger, saving the pickling liquid, and add to the bowl. Mix the pickling liquid with the remaining 1 tablespoon rice vinegar and the sesame oil. Season, add to the salad and turn everything gently until combined.

Make the omelettes following the recipe on page 82, if using.

Pile the rice salad into 4 large, shallow bowls (with or without the omelette) and an extra sprinkling of black sesame seeds and togarashi, if using.

• •

PART-TIME VARIATION

Seaweed salad with crab Swap the omelette for 200g/7oz white crabmeat. Pile it on top of the sea vegetable salad before serving.

Japanese-style omelette with summer leaves

The humble egg is such a godsend to the vegetarian kitchen, both nutritionally and for its versatility. This omelette (with a twist) comes with a simple summer leaf salad, but you could serve it on top of the Seaweed Salad (see page 80). Alternatively, it is delicious with noodles or sautéed spinach with sesame seeds and tahini stirred through it. The omelette is flavoured with the vibrant shishimi togarashi, otherwise known as Japanese seven spice. A little of this blend of orange, seaweed and spices goes a long way, and it certainly packs a flavour punch. Find it in large supermarkets or Asian grocers.

Serves **4**
Preparation time: **20 minutes**
Cooking time: **10 minutes**

8 large eggs, lightly beaten
4 tsp light soy sauce
4 large pinches shichimi togarashi
    (optional)
butter, for cooking

Summer leaves
5 large handfuls of mixed summer
    leaves, such as rocket/arugula
    leaves, watercress, baby
    spinach, tatsoi and/or baby
    chard
1 tbsp sesame oil
1 tbsp mild olive oil
juice of 1 lime
sea salt and freshly ground black
    pepper

To assemble the summer leaves, put the rocket/arugula, watercress and spinach in a serving bowl. Mix together the sesame oil, olive oil and lime juice and season with salt and pepper, to taste. Spoon the dressing over the leaves and toss until combined, then set aside until ready to serve.

To prepare the omelettes, beat 2 of the eggs in a bowl with a quarter of the soy sauce and a large pinch of togarashi, if using. If not using togarashi, season with black pepper – you shouldn't need any salt.

Melt a knob of butter in a large frying pan over a medium-low heat and swirl the pan until the butter lightly coats the base. Add the egg mixture and cook, drawing in the cooked egg from the edge and allowing the uncooked egg to run into the space. When the egg is just cooked, carefully roll the omelette up, then slip it onto a plate. Repeat to make three more omelettes – they can either be served straightaway or kept warm in a very low oven. Serve the omelettes with the summer leaves.

Chickpea pancakes with coriander yogurt

Bags of chickpea or gram flour are now readily available in larger supermarkets or Asian grocers and they're so economical to buy. This protein-rich, golden flour makes hearty pancakes or can be used to make socca, falafel, pakoras or as a crispy coating, among many other things. These pancakes are served with steamed spinach and a summery coriander yogurt – this is peak herb season after all – although, for a more substantial dish, they are also good with the Aubergine and Fresh Tomato Curry (see page 84). I also like the pancakes topped with a poached egg.

Serves **4**
Preparation time: **15 minutes**, plus 30 minutes resting
Cooking time: **10 minutes**

125g/4½oz/1 cup chickpea/gram flour
½ tsp baking powder
½ tsp ground turmeric
¾ tsp sea salt
75g/2½oz/⅓ cup plain yogurt or dairy-free alternative
1 medium-hot red chilli, deseeded and finely chopped
2 spring onions/scallions, finely chopped
coconut oil or sunflower oil, for frying
steamed spinach leaves, to serve (optional)

Coriander yogurt
150g/5½oz/⅔ cup plain yogurt or dairy-free alternative
1 garlic clove, finely chopped
juice of ½ lemon
1 large handful of fresh coriander/cilantro leaves, finely chopped
sea salt and freshly ground black pepper

To make the pancake batter, mix together the chickpea/gram flour, baking powder, turmeric and salt in a large mixing bowl. Make a well in the middle and pour in 185ml/6fl oz/¾ cup water and then add the yogurt. Whisk to make a smooth batter. Stir in the chilli and the spring onions/scallions, then leave to rest for 30 minutes.

Meanwhile, make the herbed yogurt. Mix together the yogurt with the garlic and lemon juice. Stir in the coriander/cilantro, season and set aside.

To cook the pancakes, heat enough oil to lightly coat the base of a large frying pan over a medium heat. Spoon in 3–4 tablespoons of batter per pancake and cook – about 3 at a time – for 1½ minutes on each side until cooked and golden. Remove from the pan and keep warm in a low oven. Continue, adding more oil to the pan when needed, until all the batter is used up – you should have enough for about 8 pancakes.

Serve the pancakes with steamed spinach, if you like, and the coriander yogurt by the side.

Aubergine and fresh tomato curry

〜〜〜〜〜〜〜〜〜〜〜〜〜〜〜〜〜〜〜〜〜〜〜〜〜〜〜〜〜

This is the peak season for tomatoes, when they are at their most flavoursome and plentiful. Likewise, aubergines are at their best. This simple fresh-tasting curry combines both and can be served with rice or flatbreads, or with the Chickpea Pancakes with Coriander Yogurt (see page 83) as shown in the photograph.

Serves **4**
Preparation time: **15 minutes**
Cooking time: **30 minutes**

2 tbsp coconut oil or sunflower oil
2 aubergines/eggplants, cut into
    bite-size chunks
4 large garlic cloves, finely
    chopped
5cm/2in piece of fresh root
    ginger, finely grated
1 tsp nigella seeds
1 medium-hot red chilli, deseeded
    and finely chopped
8 vine tomatoes, deseeded and
    roughly chopped
2 tbsp tomato purée/paste
1 tsp soft light brown sugar
juice of ½ lemon
salt and freshly ground black
    pepper

To serve
brown basmati rice, flatbreads
    or Chickpea Pancakes
    with Coriander Yogurt
    (see page 83)

Heat the oil in a saucepan over a medium heat, add the aubergine/eggplant and cook, stirring, for 10 minutes or until starting to colour. Reduce the heat slightly, add the garlic and ginger and cook for 1 minute, stirring, followed by the nigella seeds and the chilli. Add the tomatoes, tomato purée/paste, sugar and 125ml/4½fl oz/½ cup water and cook, part-covered, for 10–15 minutes, until the aubergine/eggplant is tender and the curry has reduced and thickened. Season and add the lemon juice.

Serve the curry with rice, flatbreads or chickpea pancakes with coriander yogurt (see page 83) on the side.

• •

PART-TIME VARIATION

Chicken and aubergine curry Replace one of the aubergines/eggplants with 2 skinless, boneless chicken breasts, cut into large bite-size chunks. Add the chicken with the tomatoes and cook as directed for 10–15 minutes until cooked through.

Beer-battered tofu tacos with pea crema

〰〰〰〰〰〰〰〰〰〰〰〰〰〰〰〰〰

Crisp, golden, batter-coated tofu, a summery pea crema and a
zingy salsa with a corn tortilla – what's not to like? If you're using
fresh peas, don't forget to save the pea pods; they make
a flavoursome light vegetable stock.

Serves **4**
Preparation time: **30 minutes**
Cooking time: **20 minutes**

165g/5¾oz/scant 1¼ cups plain/
    all-purpose flour
2 tsp cornflour/cornstarch
300ml/10½fl oz/1¼ cups light ale
4 tsp chipotle powder
4 tsp ground cumin
sunflower oil, for deep-frying
550g/1lb 4oz block of firm tofu,
    drained cut into 2cm/¾in wide
    x 1cm/½in thick fingers
sea salt and freshly ground black
    pepper

Pea crema
1 large avocado, stone removed
    and flesh scooped out
55g/2oz/⅓ cup cooked peas
4 tbsp crème fraîche
1 large garlic clove, peeled
juice of 1 lime
1 green jalapeño chilli, deseeded
    and chopped

Tomato and coriander salsa
4 vine tomatoes, deseeded and
    diced
1 handful of fresh coriander/
    cilantro leaves, chopped
½ small red onion, diced
1 green jalapeño chilli, deseeded
    and chopped
juice of ½ lime

To serve
8 corn tacos
2 Little Gem/Bibb lettuces,
    shredded
chilli sauce (optional)

To make the batter, sift the flour and cornflour/cornstarch into a
large mixing bowl. Season generously with salt and pepper. Make a
well in the middle and gradually whisk in the ale to make a smooth,
fairly thick batter. Set aside to rest. Mix together the chipotle powder
and cumin on a plate.

Blend together all the ingredients for the pea crema in a blender or
mini food processor (or mash with a fork if you like a chunky mix),
then season. Taste and add more lime, if needed.

Mix together all the ingredients for the salsa in a bowl, then season.

Place the tacos on a baking sheet and warm in the oven preheated
to 180°C/350°F/Gas 4.

To prepare the tofu, heat enough oil to half-fill a deep heavy
saucepan to 176°C/350°F (or until a cube of bread turns golden
and crisp in 40 seconds). Pat dry the tofu slices with paper towels,
making sure you get rid of as much moisture as possible, then dust
in the chipotle mix until coated all over. Dunk the tofu, one slice at a
time, into the batter until well coated, then lower it into the hot oil.
Cook 3 slices of tofu at a time for 1½–2 minutes until light golden and
crisp. Remove with a slotted spoon, drain on paper towels and keep
warm in a low oven. Repeat until you have cooked all the tofu.

To assemble, place some lettuce in a taco shell, top with 2–3 slices
of tofu and a good spoonful of the salsa, followed by the pea crema.
Finish with a dash of chilli sauce, if you like, and serve with extra
wedges of lime on the side.

· ·

PART-TIME VARIATION

Beer-battered white fish with pea crema Swap the tofu for
550g/1lb 4oz thick white fish fillets (sustainably sourced), cut into
large bite-size chunks. Pat dry and coat in the spiced flour, then the
batter. Deep-fry for 2 minutes until light golden and crisp. Serve as
suggested above.

Roasted fennel 'paella' with almond aioli

~~~~~~

If you're not a big fan of fennel, it's well worth trying it roasted. Roasting curbs its prominent aniseed flavour and the bulb takes on a delicious tender sweetness. The beauty of this rice dish is that it's cooked, for the most part, in the oven and so requires little attention. You could serve it with steamed spinach for a touch of greenness.

Serves **4**
Preparation time: **10 minutes**
Cooking time: **40 minutes**

6 tbsp olive oil

2 onions, diced

1 red pepper, deseeded and diced

4 garlic cloves, finely chopped

250g/9oz/1¼ cups paella rice

2 tsp hot smoked paprika

200ml/7fl oz/scant 1 cup dry white wine

2 fennel bulbs, cut into wedges, fronds reserved if any

1 tbsp tomato purée/paste

900ml/31fl oz/scant 4 cups good-quality hot vegetable stock

juice of 1 small lemon

1 large handful of chopped fresh flat-leaf parsley leaves

sea salt and freshly ground black pepper

Almond Aioli (see page 56), to serve

Heat 5 tablespoons of the oil in a large, heavy-based casserole over a medium-low heat. Add the onions and pepper and cook for 10 minutes, covered and stirring occasionally, until tender. Add the garlic and cook for 1 minute, then add the rice and paprika and stir until combined. Pour in the wine and let it bubble away until it evaporates and there is no smell of alcohol.

Meanwhile, preheat the oven to 180°C/350°F/Gas 4. Toss the fennel in the remaining oil, season with salt and pepper and place on a large baking sheet. Roast for 30 minutes, turning once, until tender and starting to turn golden.

To finish the rice, add the tomato purée/paste and stock and stir well, then cover with the lid and place in the oven for 20 minutes, or until the rice is cooked but not too sticky or soft. Remove from the oven, stir in the lemon juice and check the seasoning. Cover and leave to stand for 5 minutes.

Serve the rice topped with the roasted fennel, parsley and fennel fronds, if available, and a good spoonful of almond aioli.

· ·

PART-TIME VARIATION

Roasted fennel 'paella' with pancetta crisps Replace one of the fennel bulbs with 4 slices of pancetta. Place them on the baking sheet with the fennel and roast for 10 minutes, or until crisp. Remove from the oven and drain on paper towels. Serve on top of the rice with the fennel and almond aioli.

Sesame cauliflower noodles
with tahini sauce

Four of my most favourite ingredients – tahini, sesame, spinach and cauliflower – come together in this nutty noodle dish, which can be knocked together in around half an hour. The tahini creates a lovely creamy sauce, without the need for dairy. Tahini can be sensitive to temperature, so heat gently to avoid it splitting.

Serves **4**
Preparation time: **5 minutes**
Cooking time: **25 minutes**

300g/10½oz dried flat udon noodles
250g/9oz baby spinach
1 tbsp toasted sesame seeds

Tahini sauce
3 heaped tbsp tahini
3 tbsp mirin
2 tbsp light soy sauce
2 tsp caster/superfine sugar

Sesame cauliflower
2 tbsp sesame oil
2 tbsp light soy sauce
1 tsp shichimi togarashi or ½ tsp dried chilli/hot pepper flakes
1 small cauliflower, broken into florets, young outer leaves reserved
freshly ground black pepper

Preheat the oven to 190°C/375°F/Gas 5.

To prepare the cauliflower, mix together the sesame oil, soy sauce and togarashi or dried chilli/hot pepper flakes in a large mixing bowl. Season with black pepper. Add the cauliflower florets and leaves and turn until they are coated in the marinade. Tip them into a roasting pan, spread out and roast for 25 minutes, turning halfway, or until golden and cooked through. (You may need to take the leaves out after about 15 minutes if they are becoming too brown and crisp.)

Meanwhile, blend together all the ingredients for the tahini sauce until smooth and creamy.

Cook the noodles following the package directions, adding the spinach 2 minutes before the end of the cooking time. Drain, reserving 200ml/7fl oz/scant 1 cup of the cooking water.

Return the noodles and spinach to the warm pan, pour in the tahini sauce and enough of the cooking water to make a smooth, creamy sauce – you should need pretty much all of it. Using tongs, turn the noodles until coated in the sauce. Reheat briefly until warmed through, if needed. Spoon the noodles into 4 large, shallow bowls and top with the roasted cauliflower florets and leaves and sprinkle with the sesame seeds.

Roasted ratatouille with pasta

This breaks with tradition, in that the vegetables for the ratatouille are roasted rather than braised, giving them a slightly charred sweetness. There's no stirring either, which is an added bonus. Packed with veg, this is a great way of using up summer gluts, so it's well worth making in bulk; it will keep in the refrigerator for up to 3 days. The ratatouille is just as good served at room temperature as it is hot, and I also enjoy it with a spoonful of Almond Aioli (see page 56) or garlic mayonnaise, and with griddled slices of bread instead of pasta. A handful of capers thrown in with the olives wouldn't go amiss either.

Serves **4**
Preparation time: **15 minutes**
Cooking time: **50 minutes**

5 tbsp extra virgin olive oil
1 tbsp balsamic vinegar
2 tbsp chopped fresh rosemary
1 tbsp thyme leaves
1 aubergine/eggplant, cut into
    bite-size chunks
1 red pepper, deseeded and cut
    into bite-size chunks
2 red onions, trimmed and cut
    into wedges
2 courgettes/zucchini, cut into
    bite-size chunks
5 garlic cloves, unpeeled
450g/1lb small vine-ripened
    tomatoes, halved
100g/3½oz/1 cup pitted black
    olives, drained
300g/10½ oz dried penne pasta
juice of 1 lemon
1 tbsp tomato purée/paste
2 handfuls of Greek basil leaves or
    regular basil
sea salt and freshly ground black
    pepper

Preheat the oven to 200°C/400°F/Gas 6.

Combine the olive oil, vinegar, rosemary and thyme in a large mixing bowl and season generously with salt and pepper. Add the aubergine/eggplant, pepper, onions and courgettes/zucchini and turn the vegetables until well coated with the mixture. Tip the vegetables into a large, deep roasting pan, spread them out and add the garlic cloves. Roast for 25 minutes until starting to soften.

Remove the pan from the oven and take out the garlic if tender. Scatter over the tomatoes and olives and turn everything until combined. Return to the oven for another 25 minutes until the vegetables are tender and blackened in places.

Meanwhile, cook the pasta in plenty of salted boiling water, according to the package directions, until al dente. Drain, reserving 100ml/3½fl oz/scant ½ cup of the cooking water. Mix the cooking water with the lemon juice, tomato purée/paste and garlic, squeezed out of its skin.

Just before serving, add the pasta to the roasting pan with the cooking water mixture and turn until combined. Scatter over the basil before serving.

· ·
PART-TIME VARIATION

Roasted ratatouille with anchovies Halve 8 anchovies in oil and add them to the roasting pan at the same time as the olives.

Warm green bean and courgette salad

≈≈≈≈≈≈≈≈≈≈≈≈≈≈≈≈≈≈≈≈≈≈≈≈≈≈≈≈≈≈≈≈≈≈

Summer on a plate... the green beans are served warm, but they are equally good at room temperature and make a perfect picnic dish. Green beans are one of the few vegetables that aren't pleasurable to eat when undercooked or raw; you ideally want them just the right side of cooked so they are tender without being crunchy or floppy. The salad comes with a Summer Herb Cheese (see page 94), but it's also good with humous or tzatziki.

Serves **4**
Preparation time: **10 minutes**
Cooking time: **15 minutes**

225g/8oz fine green beans, trimmed
4 tbsp olive oil
1 large red onion, thinly sliced
2 yellow courgettes/zucchini (or green if you can't find them), halved and sliced
2 large garlic cloves, finely chopped
8 vine tomatoes, halved or quartered, if large
1 large handful of fresh oregano leaves, plus extra to garnish
juice of 1 lemon
sea salt and freshly ground black pepper
Summer Herb Cheese (see page 94) and crusty bread, to serve

First, steam the beans for 5 minutes or until tender. Refresh the beans under cold running water and set aside.

Meanwhile, heat 2 tablespoons of the oil in a sauté pan over a medium-low heat, add the onion and cook for 7 minutes or until softened. Add the courgettes/zucchini and garlic and cook for another 3 minutes. Stir in the tomatoes, oregano and lemon juice, reduce the heat slightly and cook for another 5 minutes until the courgettes/zucchini are just tender, but retain a little bite, and the tomatoes start to break down.

Add the cooked beans to the pan with the remaining olive oil, season with salt and pepper and warm through. Scatter over a little extra oregano before serving the bean salad with the herb cheese and some crusty bread.

Summer herb cheese

〰〰〰〰〰〰〰〰〰〰〰〰〰〰〰〰〰〰〰〰〰〰〰

Herbs are plentiful and at their culinary best at this time of year. I've used fresh chives and mint to flavour the soft cheese, but other summer herbs like basil, oregano, marjoram, flat-leaf parsley or dill would all work – it's worth experimenting with different combinations. A light lunch or snack with fresh tomatoes and crusty bread, this also makes a great accompaniment to the Warm Green Bean and Courgette Salad on page 92.

Serves **4**
Preparation time: **15 minutes**
Cooking time: **5 minutes**

250g/9oz/generous 1 cup cream or curd cheese or dairy-free alternative

6 tbsp snipped fresh chives, plus flowers if available, plus extra to serve

6 tbsp finely chopped fresh mint leaves, plus extra to serve

juice of 1 large lemon

4 tbsp mayonnaise or dairy-free alternative

2 tbsp nonpareil capers, drained and finely chopped

sea salt and freshly ground black pepper

To serve

Warm Green Bean and Courgette Salad (see page 92) or vine tomatoes, sliced

crusty bread, sliced

Mix all the ingredients for the herb cheese together, season with salt and pepper, then set aside.

Serve the herb cheese with crusty bread and the Warm Green Bean and Courgette Salad or more simply with tomatoes, sprinkled with salt and extra herbs.

• •

PART-TIME VARIATIONS

Smoked mackerel pâté Replace the herbs and capers in the soft cheese with 1 large fillet smoked mackerel, skin removed and flaked. Add the juice of 1 large lemon and 4 tbsp mayonnaise and blend until smooth and creamy. Season with salt and pepper – go easy on the salt, bearing in mind the fish is fairly salty. Scatter over a large handful of chopped flat-leaf parsley in place of the mint and chives.

Cashew cream cheese Put 125g/4½oz/1 cup cashew nuts in a bowl, pour over enough cold water to cover and leave to soak overnight, or for at least 6 hours. Drain and rinse the cashews under cold running water, then tip them into a blender. Add the juice of 1 small lemon, 1 heaped tbsp nutritional yeast flakes and 2 tbsp water, then blend until smooth and creamy. Season with salt and pepper, to taste. You can serve the cashew cream cheese plain or stir in the fresh chives and mint.

Aubergine pide

≈≈≈≈≈≈≈≈≈≈≈≈≈≈≈≈≈≈≈≈≈≈≈≈

You could describe *pide* as the Turkish cousin of the Italian pizza. It's traditionally oval shaped with the sides folded in and the top left open, but I've gone for a large rectangular-shaped one as it's ideal for sharing with others.

Serves **4**
Preparation time: **30 minutes,**
plus **2 hours rising**
Cooking time: **30 minutes**

Dough base
½ tsp caster/superfine sugar
¾ tsp fast-action/instant active dried yeast
300g/10½oz/generous 2 cups '00' flour or strong white bread flour, plus extra for dusting
1 tsp sea salt
1 tbsp extra virgin olive oil, plus extra for oiling bowl

Topping
2 tbsp extra virgin olive oil, plus extra for drizzling
1 large onion, finely chopped
1 large aubergine/eggplant, cut into small dice
1 red pepper, deseeded and diced
3 garlic cloves, finely chopped
1 heaped tsp dried oregano
2 tsp hot smoked paprika
1 heaped tbsp tomato purée/ paste
8 cherry tomatoes, halved
sea salt and freshly ground black pepper

To finish
2 handfuls of chopped fresh flat- leaf parsley leaves
1 large handful of chopped fresh mint leaves
150g/5½oz feta, crumbled (optional)

To make the pizza base, pour 100ml/3½fl oz/scant ½ cup lukewarm water into a small bowl and stir in the sugar. Sprinkle over the yeast and stir well until mixed in. Leave to stand for 15 minutes, until frothy.

Meanwhile, sift the flour and salt into a large bowl, make a well in the middle and pour in the oil. Stir the yeast mixture then add to the flour mixture. Pour in another 100ml/3½fl oz/scant ½ cup lukewarm water. Mix with a fork and then your hands to bring the mixture together into a ball – add more water if the dough is too dry or a little extra flour if too wet. Tip the dough out onto a floured work surface and knead for 5 minutes until smooth; the dough should spring back quickly when pressed. Transfer to a clean oiled bowl, cover with cling film/plastic wrap and leave until doubled in size, about 1½ hours.

Meanwhile, make the topping. Heat the oil in a frying pan over a medium heat, add the onion and fry for 5 minutes until softened. Add the aubergine/eggplant and fry for 8 minutes until tender. Add the red pepper and garlic and fry for 2 minutes, stirring. Add the oregano, smoked paprika and tomato purée/paste and heat through, adding a splash of water to loosen if necessary. Season to taste and set aside.

When the dough has risen, knock it back by pressing it with your knuckles to deflate it, then briefly knead again. Form the dough into a ball, cover with a clean cloth and set aside for a further 30 minutes.

Preheat the oven to 240°C/450°F/Gas 8. Lightly oil a large lipped baking sheet.

Roll the dough out on a floured work surface to the size of the baking sheet, then place it on the sheet, pressing the edges of the dough slightly up the sides. Spoon the topping over and scatter with the tomatoes. Drizzle with a little extra olive oil and bake for 10–12 minutes until golden. Scatter over the herbs and feta, if using, before serving.

. . . .

PART-TIME VARIATION

Aubergine and lamb pide Use only 1 small aubergine/eggplant and add 250g/9oz minced/ground lamb. Add the lamb at the same time as the aubergine/eggplant and cook, breaking up the meat, for 10 minutes until browned. Continue the recipe as above.

Chargrilled courgettes on garlic toast
with parsley relish

Chargrilling on a griddle/grill pan or barbecue does amazing things to veg, particularly summer courgettes/zucchini, peppers, aubergines/eggplants, onions and tomatoes, managing to enhance their sweetness, while lending a delicious smokiness. The same goes for chargrilled bread. This recipe marries both with a parsley salsa, and makes a perfect light, summery meal.

Serves **4**
Preparation time: **15 minutes**
Cooking time: **10 minutes**

4 courgettes/zucchini, trimmed
extra virgin olive oil, for brushing
    and drizzling
juice of ½ lemon
4–8 slices of crusty open-textured
    bread, such as ciabatta or
    sourdough, depending on size
    of loaf
2 garlic cloves, peeled and halved
    lengthways
55g/2oz vegetarian Parmesan,
    shaved (optional)
sea salt and freshly ground black
    pepper

Parsley relish
2 large handfuls of fresh flat-leaf
    parsley leaves, finely chopped
2 garlic cloves, crushed
4 tbsp extra virgin olive oil
finely grated zest of 1 unwaxed
    lemon, plus juice of 1½ lemons

Using a mandoline or sharp knife, cut the courgettes/zucchini lengthways into thin strips, about 2mm/¹⁄₁₆in thick, then brush both sides of the thin slices with oil. Heat a griddle/grill pan over a high heat (or prepare a barbecue for cooking) and chargrill the courgettes/zucchini for 5 minutes, turning once, or until tender with stripy char marks. You will have to cook the strips in batches – or barbecue them all together. Squeeze over the lemon juice, season with salt and pepper, then set aside.

Meanwhile, mix together all the ingredients for the parsley relish, season and set aside.

Next, chargrill the bread on both sides, until toasted and blackened in places – you may need to open a window! Rub the cut-side of the garlic cloves over the top of each bread slice and drizzle over a little oil. Top with the courgette/zucchini slices and a spoonful of the parsley salsa, then finish with a scattering of Parmesan, if using, and grinding of black pepper.

. . . .

PART-TIME VARIATION

Seafood on garlic toast with parsley relish Top the garlic toasts with chargrilled prawns/shrimp or squid instead of the courgettes/zucchini and Parmesan. Lightly brush 250g/9oz raw peeled tiger prawns/jumbo shrimp, or the same weight of prepared baby squid, which has been lightly scored with the point of a knife, with olive oil. Season with salt, pepper and smoked paprika before chargrilling or barbecuing; it should take about 2–3 minutes for the prawns/shrimp and 1–2 minutes for the squid. Serve as suggested, above. You could also swap the parsley for Greek basil in the relish.

Courgette koftas in vine tomato sauce

≈≈≈≈≈≈≈≈≈≈≈≈≈≈≈≈≈≈≈≈≈≈≈≈≈≈≈≈≈≈≈≈

Seasonal, slightly overripe vine tomatoes make the best-tasting fresh sauce. Give tomatoes a good sniff before you buy them and choose fragrant ones that are still on the vine – if there is no tomatoey aroma, then chances are they'll have little flavour either. The secret to the success of these koftas is to squeeze as much water out of the courgettes/zucchini as possible to ensure they hold their shape when cooked.

Serves **4**
Preparation time: **20 minutes**,
plus 20 minutes salting
Cooking time: **55 minutes**

2 courgettes/zucchini, coarsely grated
1 onion, quartered
2 garlic cloves, peeled
400g/14oz can green lentils, drained
1 egg, lightly beaten
40g/1½oz/⅔ cup vegetarian Parmesan cheese, finely grated, plus extra to serve
1 tbsp chopped fresh oregano or 1½ tsp dried
115g/4½oz/2 cups slightly stale fresh breadcrumbs
2 tbsp plain/all-purpose flour
1 handful of basil leaves
sea salt and freshly ground black pepper
pasta, rice or crusty bread, to serve

Tomato sauce
3 tbsp olive oil, plus extra for frying
2 garlic cloves, finely chopped
2 large bay leaves
900g/2lb ripe vine tomatoes, deseeded and chopped, vine stalks reserved
200ml/7fl oz/scant 1 cup good-quality vegetable stock
½ tsp caster/superfine sugar

Place the courgettes/zucchini in a colander over a large shallow bowl. Sprinkle with salt and leave for 20 minutes to remove any excess water, then rinse briefly and squeeze dry in a clean dish towel.

Meanwhile, start the tomato sauce. Heat the olive oil in a saucepan over a medium-low heat. Add the garlic and bay leaves and cook for 1 minute until softened, but not coloured. Add the tomatoes, vine stalks, stock and sugar and bring almost to the boil, then reduce the heat to very low, cover, and simmer for 50 minutes, or until reduced. Season with salt and pepper, to taste, and remove the vine stalks.

Preheat the oven to 200°C/400°F/Gas 6. Line a baking sheet with baking paper and lightly oil.

To finish the koftas, put the onion, garlic cloves and lentils into a food processor and blend to a coarse, rough paste. Spoon the paste into a mixing bowl and stir in the courgettes/zucchini, egg, Parmesan, oregano, breadcrumbs and flour until well combined. Season generously with salt and pepper. Form the mixture into about 28 walnut-sized balls and arrange on the prepared baking sheet. Brush the koftas with oil, then bake for 25–30 minutes until golden.

Arrange the baked koftas on top of the tomato sauce with a sprinkling of basil leaves. Serve with pasta, rice or crusty bread.

· ·

PART-TIME VARIATION

Courgette and beef kofta in vine tomato sauce Swap one of the courgettes/zucchini with 150g/5½oz lean minced/ground beef. Stir the meat into the blended onion, garlic and lentil paste at the same time as the other ingredients. Season generously with salt and pepper, then follow the directions for shaping and cooking as above.

Sweetcorn polenta
with roast peppers and beans

Instant fine polenta/cornmeal cooks much quicker than the coarse-grained alternative – cooking times vary by brand, so do check. While it is baking, make the most of the oven to roast some peppers. You can also use the spent corn cobs as a base for a vegetable stock – simply simmer them in water for 20 minutes.

Serves **4**
Preparation time: **15 minutes,**
plus cooling
Cooking time: **45 minutes**

2 red peppers, deseeded and cut into long strips
4 tbsp extra virgin olive oil, plus extra for brushing/drizzling
150g/5½oz runner beans, thinly sliced diagonally
4 garlic cloves, finely chopped
6 vine tomatoes, chopped into large chunks
2 tbsp fresh oregano leaves or 2 tsp dried
400g/14oz can haricot/navy beans, drained
juice of 1 lemon
1 large handful of basil leaves
sea salt and freshly ground black pepper

Sweetcorn polenta
2 sweetcorn cobs, husks removed (about 450g/1lb total weight)
2 tsp vegetable bouillon powder
200g/7oz/1⅓ cups instant fine polenta/cornmeal
25g/1oz/2 tbsp butter

Cook the sweetcorn cobs in boiling water for 5 minutes or until the kernels are just tender. Remove the cobs from the pan, reserving the water, refresh under cold running water, then slice off the kernels. Crush the kernels slightly with the back of a fork and set aside.

Measure the corn cooking water – you need 800ml/28fl oz/scant 3½ cups (top up with extra hot water, if necessary). Return the water to the pan, stir in the bouillon powder and bring to the boil. Gradually pour in the polenta, stirring constantly with a balloon whisk and cook for 5–8 minutes or until thick and smooth with no hint of graininess. Switch to a wooden spoon when the polenta becomes too thick to stir with the whisk. Remove from the heat and stir in the butter and cooked corn. Spoon the mixture into a deep baking sheet lined with cling film/plastic wrap and spread out with a wet palette knife until about 1cm/½in thick. Leave to cool.

When cool, cut the polenta into 4 pieces, then cut each piece into 2 triangles. Meanwhile, preheat the oven to 200°C/400°F/Gas 6.

Toss the red pepper in a little oil, spread out in a roasting pan and roast for 25 minutes or until tender. Use a spatula to transfer the polenta triangles to a second larger baking sheet where they will have space around them, brush with oil and bake for 15 minutes until slightly crisp.

Meanwhile, steam the runner beans until just tender, then refresh under cold running water and set aside.

Heat the oil in a sauté pan over a medium heat, add the garlic and cook for 1 minute. Stir in the tomatoes, oregano and haricot/navy beans and cook for 5 minutes, stirring occasionally, until the tomatoes start to break down. When the peppers are ready, you can either peel off their skins (letting them cool a little first) or add straight to the pan with the runner beans, lemon juice and 150ml/5fl oz/⅔ cup water. Season generously with salt and pepper and warm through.

Serve the bean mixture on top of the polenta triangles with an extra drizzle of olive oil, if liked, and a scattering of basil leaves.

Barbecue feast

....

MENU

Serves 4

°°

Jackfruit kebabs with tahini yogurt sauce

°°

Charred aubergines

°°

Corn with chilli and lime

°°

Chargrilled lettuce with miso dressing

°°

Barbecued baby carrots with avocado and ginger

There's a distinct Middle-Eastern feel to this barbecue menu – you can choose to cook it in its entirety or just select a dish or two. If jackfruit is new to you, then this tropical fruit is well worth trying. It makes a versatile vegan alternative to meat, with a texture akin to pulled pork or shredded chicken when marinated and cooked. Marinating is a must as it is quite neutral in flavour in its natural state. The charred aubergine/eggplant salad takes its inspiration from a similar dish tasted in Turkey a few years back and has become a favourite ever since. Meanwhile, the chargrilled lettuce is sure to win over non-lettuce fans with its wonderful smokiness and crisp texture. Look for a firm crunchy lettuce, such as Little Gem/ Bibb, Cos or romaine, as you want it to retain its texture. A barbecue wouldn't be a barbecue without corn and these cobs come with a zingy lime and chilli dressing, while the summer season's baby carrots taste sweet and fresh and deliciously smoky. Try to find carrots of varying colours, if you can, although orange ones are not to be sniffed at if they're the only ones to be had.

Jackfruit kebabs with tahini yogurt sauce

Preparation time: 20 minutes, plus at least 1 hour marinating | Cooking time: 10 minutes

560g/1lb 4oz can jackfruit in brine, drained (260g/9¼oz drained weight), rinsed, cut into bite-size chunks and tough cores trimmed, if needed
2 red peppers, halved, deseeded and cut into large bite-size chunks
4 small red onions, peeled, root ends trimmed, each cut into 6 wedges
2 courgettes/zucchini, cut into thick slices
16 bay leaves (optional)
flatbreads and fresh coriander/cilantro leaves, to serve

Marinade
2 tsp ground cumin
2½ tbsp harissa paste
1½ tsp dried oregano
3 garlic cloves, crushed
juice of 1 large lemon
2 tbsp olive oil
sea salt and freshly ground black pepper

Tahini yogurt sauce
150ml/5½fl oz/¾ cup Greek-style plain yogurt
3 tbsp tahini
juice of 1 large lemon
1 large garlic clove, crushed

Prepare your barbecue for cooking. Alternatively, you could also cook these kebabs on a preheated griddle/grill pan or under a high grill/broiler. If using bamboo skewers, soak for 30 minutes in water before using to stop them burning.

Mix together all the ingredients for the marinade. Season with salt and pepper.

Lightly flatten the jackfruit pieces with the blade of a knife so the edges splay out slightly to look more 'meat-like'. Thread the jackfruit, red peppers, onions and courgettes/zucchini, occasionally interspersing them with a bay leaf, if using, onto 8 metal or bamboo skewers. Place the skewers in a large shallow dish and generously brush over the marinade, leaving some for cooking. Leave to marinate for at least 1 hour, or longer if time allows.

Mix together all the ingredients for the tahini yogurt sauce and set aside.

Barbecue (or chargrill/grill) the kebabs, occasionally turning them and brushing with extra marinade, for 10 minutes or until cooked and charred in places. Serve the kebabs with warmed flatbreads, the tahini sauce and a sprinkling of coriander/cilantro leaves.

· ·
PART-TIME VARIATION
Chicken kebabs with tahini yogurt sauce Replace the jackfruit with 260g/9¼oz skinless, boneless chicken thighs, cut into bite-size chunks (or you could go half and half).

Charred aubergine salad

Preparation time: 10 minutes | Cooking time: 20 minutes

2 medium aubergines/eggplants
5 tbsp extra virgin olive oil
3 garlic cloves, finely chopped
2 tsp hot smoked paprika
1 tsp pul biber (Aleppo pepper) or ½ tsp
    dried chilli/hot pepper flakes
2 tsp cumin seeds
6 vine tomatoes, deseeded and diced
pinch of sugar
squeeze of lemon juice
sea salt and freshly ground black pepper
fresh coriander/cilantro leaves, chopped,
    to garnish

Prepare your barbecue for cooking. Place the aubergines/eggplants directly on the barbecue rack and cook for about 20 minutes, turning occasionally, or until the skins have blackened and the insides are tender. When cool enough to handle, cut in half, scoop out the flesh and finely chop.

Meanwhile, heat the oil in a frying pan over a medium-low heat, add the garlic and fry for 1 minute. Add the spices, stirring until fragrant, then add the tomatoes, sugar and 2 tablespoons water. Cook, stirring, for 8 minutes, until the tomatoes have started to break down. Add to the aubergine/eggplant with a squeeze of lemon. Season and scatter with coriander/cilantro. Serve warm or at room temperature.

Corn with chilli and lime

Preparation time: 5 minutes | Cooking time: 25 minutes

2 tbsp softened butter or coconut oil
½ tsp dried chilli/hot pepper flakes
juice of 1 lime
¼ tsp sea salt
4 corn cobs, husks pulled back or removed

Prepare your barbecue for cooking. Mash together the butter or coconut oil, dried chilli/hot pepper flakes, lime juice and salt.

Wrap each corn cob in a double layer of foil and barbecue for 20–25 minutes, turning occasionally, until tender and a little charred. If you'd like the cobs a bit more charred, remove them from their foil parcels and place directly on the barbecue for a few minutes, turning occasionally.

Alternatively, cook the corn in boiling water for 5 minutes and drain, then chargrill in a hot griddle/grill pan or over the flame of a hob. Brush the corn with the butter or oil mixture and serve hot.

Chargrilled lettuce with miso dressing

Preparation time: 5 minutes | Cooking time: 7 minutes

6 small Little Gem/Bibb lettuces, halved
    lengthways
olive oil, for brushing

Miso dressing
3 tbsp white miso
5 tsp runny honey
3 tbsp extra virgin olive oil
freshly ground black pepper

Prepare your barbecue for cooking. Lightly brush the lettuces all over with oil, then barbecue (or chargrill) for 5–7 minutes, turning once or twice, until blackened in places and tender.

Meanwhile, mix together all the ingredients for the dressing with 2 tablespoons hot water until combined.

Arrange the lettuces on a serving platter and spoon the dressing over the top.

. . . .
PART-TIME VARIATIONS
Barbecued meat or seafood The miso dressing would also be delicious spooned over barbecued cuts of meat, poultry, white fish, king prawns/jumbo shrimp and squid.

Barbecued baby carrots with avocado and ginger

Preparation time: 10 minutes | Cooking time: 15–20 minutes

12 mixed-colour heirloom baby carrots, or 6
    medium carrots, scrubbed and trimmed
extra virgin olive oil, for brushing
1 large ripe avocado, halved, stone and skin
    removed, cut into bite-size chunks
1 handful of fresh mint leaves
1 green serrano chilli, deseeded and thinly
    sliced

Dressing
1 tsp coriander seeds, toasted
3 tbsp extra virgin olive oil
juice of 1 lemon
2 tsp finely grated fresh root ginger
1 tsp runny honey
sea salt and freshly ground black pepper

Prepare your barbecue for cooking. Lightly brush the carrots with oil and barbecue for 10–15 minutes, turning occasionally, until charred in places and just tender. Alternatively, roast in an oven preheated to 200°C/400°F/Gas 6 for 20 minutes.

Crush the coriander seeds using a pestle and mortar. Tip into a bowl and stir in the rest of the ingredients for the dressing.

Arrange the carrots in a serving dish and top with the avocado. Spoon enough of the dressing over to lightly coat, then finish with the mint leaves and sliced chilli on top.

Sesame empanada pie

〜〜〜〜〜〜〜〜〜〜〜〜〜〜〜〜〜〜〜〜〜〜〜〜〜

There are many versions of empanada and this is based on one from Galicia, a stunning part of northern Spain. It's a large pie, rather than the small pasty shape more often seen in other parts of Spain as well as Argentina. Baked in the oven, rather than fried, the pie is perfect fare for a picnic or summer lunch.

Serves **6**
Preparation time: **25 minutes**, plus cooling
Cooking time: **40 minutes**

450g/14oz/scant 3½ cups plain/all-purpose flour, plus extra for dusting
1 tsp sea salt
2 tsp baking powder
7 tbsp olive oil, plus extra for greasing
1 large egg, lightly beaten, plus 1 for glazing
2 tsp sesame seeds

Filling
3 onions, sliced
1 red pepper, deseeded and chopped
75g/2½oz/¾ cup pitted black olives, sliced
1 tbsp nonpareil capers, drained, rinsed and patted dry
1 tsp smoked paprika
1½ tsp dried oregano
4 vine tomatoes, chopped
2 tbsp tomato purée/paste
5 hard-boiled eggs, peeled and sliced
sea salt and freshly ground black pepper

To make the pastry, sift the flour, salt and baking powder into a large mixing bowl. Make a well in the middle and add 5 tablespoons of the olive oil, the egg and 135ml/4½fl oz/generous ½ cup water. Using a fork, gradually draw the dry ingredients into the wet, then use your hands to bring everything together and knead briefly to make a soft ball of dough. Wrap in cling film/plastic wrap and chill until needed.

To make the filling, heat the remaining oil in a large frying pan over a medium heat, add the onions and fry for 5 minutes. Add the red pepper and cook for another 5 minutes until the onions and pepper have softened. Stir in the olives, capers, smoked paprika, oregano, tomatoes and tomato purée/paste. Season and cook for another 5 minutes, until reduced and thickened. Leave to cool.

Preheat the oven to 190°C/375°F/Gas 5 and grease a 31cm/12½in loose-bottomed tart pan with oil.

Divide the pastry into two-thirds for the base and sides, and one-third for the top. Roll out the larger piece of pastry on a lightly floured work surface until large enough to line the base and sides of the pan with a slight overhang. Spoon the cooled filling mixture into the pastry case and top with a layer of sliced hard-boiled eggs.

Roll out the remaining pastry into a round large enough to cover the top of the pie. Slightly fold the pastry base over the top, trim any excess pastry and pinch together to seal. Prick the top a few times with a fork, brush with beaten egg and sprinkle over the sesame seeds. Bake for 25 minutes or until golden and cooked. Leave in the pan for 5 minutes, then remove and serve cut into slices.

• •

PART-TIME VARIATION

Tuna empanada pie Replace the hard-boiled eggs with 1 x 160g/5¾oz can tuna in olive oil. Drain the tuna, reserving the oil. Use the oil to fry the onions, then either mix the tuna into the tomato filling mixture or spoon it on top in the same way as the eggs.

Avocado, pea and mint pasta

~~~~~~

Avocado makes a surprisingly good, creamy, nutritious sauce – and you couldn't get more summery than the classic combination of mint and pea. Put together, you have a simple, no-fuss sauce for pasta. Make the sauce just before serving, when it is at its best.

Serves **4**
Preparation time: **10 minutes**
Cooking time: **15 minutes**

400g/14oz dried spaghetti
250g/9oz/1⅔ cups shelled peas, fresh or frozen
1 ripe avocado, halved, stone removed and flesh scooped out
juice of ½ lemon
5 tbsp chopped fresh mint leaves
1 large garlic clove, peeled
sea salt and freshly ground black pepper

To serve
vegetarian Parmesan cheese, finely grated (optional)
dried chilli/hot pepper flakes, to taste

Cook the pasta in plenty of salted boiling water following the package directions. Drain, saving 150ml/5fl oz/⅔ cup of the cooking water, and return the pasta to the pan.

Meanwhile, steam the peas until just tender, then refresh under cold running water.

Blend half of the cooked peas with the avocado, lemon juice, 3 tablespoons of the mint, 100ml/3½fl oz/scant ½ cup of the pasta cooking water and the garlic until smooth and creamy. Season to taste.

Stir the sauce into the pasta with the reserved peas and warm through briefly. Add the rest of the mint and more of the cooking water, if needed, then check the seasoning. Spoon into 4 large, shallow bowls and grate over Parmesan, if using, then sprinkle with some dried chilli/hot pepper flakes. Add a little extra mint, if you like.

Tomato tarts with preserved lemon relish

Super-easy and super-looking! Tomatoes are at their flavoursome best now, especially those allowed to ripen on the vine before picking. To keep things simple, I've used a ready-made, all-butter puff pastry and red cherry tomatoes, but you could experiment with different-coloured tomatoes – yellow, orange, black – whatever you can find. Serve with a green salad and boiled and buttered new potatoes.

Serves **6**
Preparation time: **20 minutes**
Cooking time: **25 minutes**

1 tbsp extra virgin olive oil, plus extra for brushing

2 large echalion/banana shallots, finely chopped

2 tsp fresh thyme leaves, plus extra to garnish

320g/11¼oz pack all-butter, ready-rolled puff pastry, chilled

140g/5oz vine cherry tomatoes, halved (save the vine stalk for adding to sauces and stews)

sea salt and freshly ground black pepper

Preserved lemon relish

4 preserved lemons from a jar, drained

4 tsp apple cider vinegar

2–4 tsp runny honey

2 tbsp extra virgin olive oil

40g/1½oz/⅓ cup unsalted roasted shelled pistachios, roughly chopped

Preheat the oven to 200°C/400°F/Gas 6. Line 2 baking sheets with baking paper.

Heat the olive oil in a large frying pan over a medium heat, add the shallots and fry for 8 minutes, until softened but not coloured – reduce the heat slightly if they start to brown. Stir in the thyme at the end of cooking.

Remove the pastry from the refrigerator, unroll the sheet and divide into 6 pieces. Score a border, about 1cm/½in from the edge, around each piece and prick the base of each one a few times with a fork. Arrange the pastry bases on the lined baking sheets. Spoon on the onions, then top with the tomatoes, arranging them in lines cut-side down. Lightly brush the tomatoes and pastry edges with olive oil and season the tops with salt and pepper. Bake for 20–25 minutes, until the pastry is cooked and golden.

Meanwhile, scoop out and discard the flesh from the preserved lemons. Finely chop the skins and mix with the cider vinegar and honey with the olive oil until combined. Taste and add more honey if you feel it needs to be sweeter. Just before serving, add the pistachios so they keep their crunch.

Scatter a little extra thyme over the tarts before serving with the preserved lemon relish.

AUTUMN

Autumn

As we ease into darker nights and colder days, our choice of what we like to eat shifts to more comforting foods and we begin to crave more substantial, warming dishes like soups, stews and roasts. Autumn/fall welcomes a bumper harvest of richly coloured vegetables, from golden-hued squash and pumpkins and earthy brown mushrooms to deep magenta beetroot/beets and leafy-green chard. There are chestnuts, hazelnuts, apples and pears, too – a harmonious collection of fresh foods whose tastes, colours and textures complement each other when used together.

Seasonal vegetables:

Aubergine/eggplant (in season early autumn/fall)

Beetroot/beets (peak)

Broccoli (in season)

Cabbage, green/red/white/Savoy (peak)

Carrot (in season)

Cauliflower (peak)

Cavolo nero (peak)

Chard (in season)

Garlic (in season)

Kale (peak)

Leek (peak)

Mushroom (peak)

Onion (peak)

Onion, spring/scallion (in season)

Parsnip (in season)

Pepper and chilli (in season)

Potato, main crop (peak)

Pumpkin and squash (peak)

Radicchio/endive (in season)

Radish (in season)

Rocket/arugula (in season)

Shallot (peak)

Spinach (in season)

Sweetcorn (in season)

Sweet potato (peak)

Tomato (in season)

Turnip (peak)

Watercress (in season)

Carrot, ginger and lentil soup
with carrot crisps

Warming and comforting, a bowl of this hearty, nutritious soup is a go-to when the weather is chilly and I'm looking for sustenance. The carrot crisps are a great way to use up carrot peelings. When roasted, they add crunch and a contrast in texture to the smooth soup – they also make a healthy snack.

Serves **4**
Preparation time: **15 minutes**
Cooking time: **30 minutes**

550g/1lb 4oz carrots, scrubbed
2 tbsp olive oil, plus extra for
    drizzling
1 large onion, roughly chopped
1 celery stalk, thinly sliced
2 tsp ground coriander
½ tsp ground turmeric
1 thumb-size piece of fresh root
    ginger, peeled and finely
    grated
175g/6oz/1 cup split red lentils,
    rinsed well
2 bay leaves
1.2 litres/40fl oz/5 cups good-
    quality hot vegetable stock
juice of ½ lemon
sea salt and freshly ground black
    pepper
4 tbsp thick plain yogurt and
    ½ tsp nigella seeds, to serve

Preheat the oven to 180°C/350°F/Gas 4.

Start by making the carrot crisps. Using a vegetable peeler, peel away the skin of the carrots into long, thin strips. Toss the carrot strips in a drizzle of oil and place in an even layer on a large baking sheet. Roast for 15 minutes or until crisp and golden, turning once – keep an eye on them as they can easily burn. Remove from the heat, transfer to a plate lined with paper towels and leave to cool and crisp up further.

Meanwhile, cut the peeled carrots into chunks. Heat the oil in a large heavy-based saucepan over a medium-low heat, add the onion and cook for 5 minutes, until softened. Add the celery and carrots and cook for another 2 minutes. Stir in the spices followed by the lentils and bay leaves, then pour in the stock. Stir and bring to the boil, then reduce the heat to low, part-cover the pan with a lid and simmer for 20 minutes, or until the lentils and carrots are tender.

Using a hand-held stick/immersion blender, blend the soup until smooth. Stir in the lemon juice and season with salt and pepper, to taste.

Ladle the soup into bowls, then top with a good spoonful of yogurt, a few nigella seeds and the carrot crisps.

Cauliflower, coconut and lemongrass soup

Cauliflower marries well with anything cheesy, milky or creamy, whether dairy or dairy-free. This light, fragrant soup features coconut milk and is delicately flavoured with lemongrass, ginger and lime. For a contrast in flavour and texture, save some of the cauliflower florets to make a topping – fry or roast and sprinkle on top of the soup with chilli and coriander.

Serves **4–6**
Preparation time: **15 minutes**
Cooking time: **20 minutes**

1 large cauliflower, outer leaves removed, pale green inner leaves reserved
2 tbsp coconut oil
2 onions, chopped
3 garlic cloves, peeled
4cm/1½in piece of fresh root ginger, peeled and cut into matchsticks
1 large potato, about 350g/12oz total weight, peeled and cut into chunks
1 tsp ground turmeric
1 litre/35fl oz/4¼ cups good-quality hot vegetable stock
400g/14oz can coconut milk
3 large lemongrass stalks, outer layers removed and reserved, inside finely chopped
juice of 1 lime
1 medium-hot red chilli, deseeded and thinly sliced
1 handful of fresh coriander/cilantro leaves, chopped
sea salt and freshly ground black pepper

Set aside 140g/5oz of the cauliflower for the topping. Roughly chop the remaining cauliflower, including the stalks and leaves.

Heat half of the coconut oil in a large saucepan over a medium heat, add the onions and cook for 5 minutes, stirring, until softened but not coloured. Add the garlic, ginger, potato, chopped cauliflower, turmeric and stock and bring to the boil. Reduce the heat, stir in the coconut milk and lemongrass, including the reserved outer layers, and simmer for 15 minutes until the vegetables are tender.

Meanwhile, make the topping. Chop the reserved cauliflower into very small florets. Heat the remaining coconut oil in a frying pan over a medium heat, add the cauliflower and stir-fry for 5 minutes or until golden and slightly crisp. (You could also roast it at 180°C/350°F/Gas 4 for 20 minutes.)

Remove and discard the large lemongrass layers from the soup. Using a stick/immersion blender, blend the soup until smooth and creamy. Add the lime juice and season generously with salt and pepper. Serve the soup topped with the crispy cauliflower, chilli and coriander/cilantro.

Crispy mushroom pancakes
with hoisin sauce

A meat-free take on the classic Chinese crispy duck pancakes, with paper-thin pancakes topped with a smear of hoisin sauce, crisp fried mushrooms and slivers of spring onion/scallion and cucumber. I've given a recipe for homemade hoisin, which will keep in the refrigerator for up to 2 weeks, but of course you could go for a ready-made sauce instead.

Serves **4**
Preparation time: **25 minutes**
Cooking time: **30 minutes**

2 tbsp sunflower oil, plus extra for brushing
400g/14oz chestnut/cremini mushrooms, thinly sliced
12 Chinese pancakes
5 spring onions/scallions, finely shredded
1 small cucumber, quartered, deseeded and cut into thin matchsticks
1 small turnip, peeled and cut into thin matchsticks

Hoisin sauce
2 tbsp sesame oil
2 garlic cloves, crushed
5 tbsp dark soy sauce
3 tbsp soft light brown sugar
2 tbsp rice vinegar
2 tsp chilli sauce
¾ tsp Chinese 5-spice powder
2 tbsp smooth peanut butter
freshly ground black pepper

To make the hoisin sauce, heat the sesame oil in a small pan over a low heat and cook the garlic for 2 minutes. Stir in the soy sauce, sugar, vinegar, chilli sauce and Chinese 5-spice along with 1 tablespoon water. Remove from the heat, stir in the peanut butter and season with pepper – add a splash more water if the sauce is very thick. Set aside to cool.

To make the crispy mushrooms, heat the sunflower oil in a large frying pan over a medium-high heat. Add the mushrooms and fry for 12–15 minutes until any liquid in the pan has evaporated and they turn crisp and golden. Stir in 4 tablespoons of the hoisin sauce and warm through until it becomes sticky and glossy and coats the mushrooms.

Prepare the pancakes according to the package directions and keep warm.

To serve, spoon the remaining hoisin sauce into a bowl and place the spring onions/scallions, cucumber and turnip on a plate. To assemble, spread a warm pancake with a little hoisin, then top with the mushrooms, and a few slices of spring onion/scallion, cucumber and turnip. Roll up before eating. It's best to lay everything out on the table and let everyone help themselves...

. . . .
PART-TIME VARIATION

Crispy duck pancakes with hoisin sauce Replace the mushrooms with 2 skinless duck breasts, cut into thin strips. Heat the sunflower oil in the frying pan over a medium heat, add the duck breasts and stir-fry for 3–4 minutes until cooked through. Add 4 tablespoons hoisin sauce and stir-fry for another 1 minute until the duck is coated in the sauce. Serve as directed above.

Brunch

························

MENU
Serves 4

°°

Bread, kale and smoked paprika frittata

°°

Smoky beans

°°

Orange and pomegranate salad with mint and lime

Brunch is such a civilized meal – it suggests relaxed, unhurried eating to be enjoyed with family and friends. This menu particularly appeals as it's largely made up of leftovers and storecupboard ingredients. The frittata is an eggy variation of the Spanish dish *migas* and makes use of leftover, slightly stale bread. The beans are a riff on the beloved canned baked bean and are flavoured with smoked paprika. Fresh and vibrant, the orange and pomegranate fruit salad is perfect for cleansing the palate after the savoury dishes, and gives a burst of vitamin C – just right for the autumn/fall months, when we often need a boost.

Bread, kale and smoked paprika frittata

Preparation time: 10 minutes, plus 15 minutes soaking | Cooking time: 25 minutes

300g/10½oz slightly stale country-style, open-textured bread, such as sourdough or ciabatta, cut into large bite-size chunks
200ml/7fl oz/scant 1 cup milk
3 tbsp extra virgin olive oil
25g/1oz/2 tbsp butter
1 onion, finely chopped
125g/4½oz kale, tough stalks removed, leaves torn into pieces
1 large handful of coriander/cilantro or parsley leaves, chopped
1 tsp hot or mild smoked paprika (to taste)
4 eggs, lightly beaten
salt and freshly ground black pepper
Tahini Yogurt Sauce (see page 101), to serve (optional)

In a large shallow bowl, soak the bread in the milk for 15 minutes until softened.

Meanwhile, heat the oil and butter in a large ovenproof frying pan over a medium heat, add the onion and cook, stirring often, for 5 minutes until softened. Give the bread a slight squeeze to remove any excess milk and add to the pan. Cook, pressing the bread down with a spatula and turning occasionally, for 8–10 minutes until the bread starts to turn golden and slightly crisp on the outside, but is still moist in the middle.

Preheat the grill/broiler to high.

Add the kale to the pan and cook for another 3 minutes, stirring occasionally, until the kale wilts and starts to turn crisp in places. Reduce the heat to low and stir in the herbs, then spread the mixture evenly over the base of the pan.

Beat the paprika into the eggs and season with salt and pepper. Pour the mixture over the contents of the pan and cook for 4 minutes or until the base is cooked and light golden, while the top is still slightly runny. Place the pan under the hot grill/broiler for 2 minutes or until the egg is just cooked. Serve cut into wedges with the tahini yogurt sauce, if liked, on the side.

Smoky beans

Preparation time: 10 minutes | Cooking time: 12 minutes

2 tbsp extra virgin olive oil
2 garlic cloves, finely chopped
splash of white wine, about 80ml/2½fl
 oz/⅓ cup (optional)
2 x 400g/14oz cans cannellini beans,
 drained
6 vine tomatoes, roughly chopped
2 tbsp tomato purée/paste
1½ tsp hot or mild smoked paprika
 (to taste)
juice of 1 lemon
salt and freshly ground black pepper
1 handful of parsley leaves, chopped,
 to garnish

Heat the olive oil in a saucepan over a medium-low heat, add the garlic and cook, stirring to prevent it burning, for 1 minute. Add the wine, if using, and cook briefly until reduced and there is no aroma of alcohol.

Stir in the beans, tomatoes, tomato purée/paste, paprika and 60ml/2½fl oz/¼ cup water and bring almost to the boil. Reduce the heat, part-cover with a lid, and simmer for 10 minutes until the tomatoes have broken down and the sauce has reduced and thickened. Stir in the lemon juice, season and warm through, adding a splash more water if the sauce is very dry. Serve sprinkled with parsley.

• •

PART-TIME VARIATION

Smoky beans with ham hock Stir 75g/2½oz pulled ham hock, flaked, into the beans with the lemon juice and warm through.

Orange and pomegranate salad with mint and lime

Preparation time: 15 minutes

4 oranges, such as Valencia
1 pomegranate
honey, for drizzling
juice of 1 lime
1 handful of fresh mint leaves
25g/1oz/generous ¼ cup toasted flaked
  almonds
Greek yogurt or dairy-free alternative,
  to serve

To prepare the oranges, cut a slice off the top and bottom of each fruit so they sit flat on a plate. Using a sharp knife, work your way round each orange to remove the skin and pith. Slice the oranges into thin rounds and arrange the fruit and any juices on a large serving plate.

To prepare the pomegranate, starting from the crown, cut the fruit into quarters over a bowl to catch any juices. Bend each quarter back to release the seeds into the bowl and remove any white membrane.

Scatter the pomegranate seeds over the orange and spoon over any juices. Cover and refrigerate until ready to serve.

Before serving, drizzle with honey, add a squeeze of lime juice and top with mint leaves. Scatter the flaked almonds over and serve with Greek yogurt on the side.

Parsnip latkes with beetroot horseradish cream

~~~~~~

We have a mixed love of parsnips in our house. That said, these latkes were a hands-down triumph with all. The bonus of using parsnip to make latkes, rather than the more usual potato, is that it is drier in texture, resulting in a crisp, golden fritter. Serve topped with a poached or fried egg, or see the suggestions below, to make a more substantial dish.

Serves **4**
Preparation time: **20 minutes**
Cooking time: **20 minutes**

500g/1lb 2oz parsnips, peeled
    and coarsely grated
1 red onion, coarsely grated
2½ tbsp self-raising/self-rising
    flour
2 eggs
sunflower oil, for frying
sea salt and freshly ground black
    pepper
rocket/arugula leaves, to serve

Beetroot horseradish cream
5 tbsp crème fraîche
1½ tbsp horseradish sauce
juice of ½ lemon
100g/3½oz raw beetroot/beets,
    peeled and coarsely grated

To make the beetroot horseradish cream, mix together all the ingredients and season with salt and pepper, to taste. Set aside.

Put the grated parsnips into a mixing bowl. Squeeze the grated onion in paper towels to remove any excess water, then add to the parsnips. Stir in the flour. Lightly beat the eggs and stir into the vegetable mixture, then season well with salt and pepper.

Heat enough oil to generously coat the base of a large frying pan over a medium heat. Place a large spoonful (about 50ml/2fl oz/ 3 tbsp) of the latke mixture into the pan and flatten with a spatula to a thin round, about 7.5cm/3in in diameter. Cook 3 latkes at a time for 2 minutes on each side, or until crisp and golden on the outside and cooked through. Remove to drain on paper towels and keep warm in a low oven while you cook the rest of the mixture – it makes 12 latkes in total.

Divide the latkes between 4 serving plates, top each with a handful of rocket/arugula leaves and add a good spoonful of the beetroot horseradish cream.

. . . .

PART-TIME VARIATION

Topping ideas Poached or fried egg; pan-fried slices of smoked tofu; grilled salmon or mackerel fillet; grilled slices of pancetta; leftover cooked roast chicken or beef.

Roasted broccoli and squash with smashed beans

~~~~~~

Canned beans are such a storecupboard asset – they're handy, versatile and require little preparation. However, if time allows, I sometimes like to cook up a batch of dried beans (see page 12). You'll need about 300g/10½oz/1¾ cups dried beans for this dish. This is peak Calabrese broccoli season, but if you've grown weary of it steamed or boiled, try roasting – it takes on a new lease of life.

Serves **4**
Preparation time: **20 minutes**
Cooking time: **25 minutes**

1 butternut squash, about
    900g/2lb, peeled, deseeded
    (seeds reserved), cut into large
    bite-size chunks
2 tbsp extra virgin olive oil
300g/10½oz broccoli florets
150g/5½oz feta cheese,
    crumbled
2–4 tbsp Dukkah (see page 146
    or use ready-made or ras el
    hanout)
sea salt and freshly ground black
    pepper

Smashed beans
5 tbsp extra virgin olive oil
3 large garlic cloves, finely
    chopped
3 x 400g/14oz cans white beans
    (such as butter/lima beans),
    drained
finely grated zest of ½ large
    unwaxed lemon, plus juice of 1,
    plus extra for squeezing over
250ml/9fl oz/1 cup good-quality
    vegetable stock, plus extra
    if needed

Preheat the oven to 190°C/375°F/Gas 5.

Place the squash and reserved seeds on a baking sheet and toss in half of the oil. Season with salt and pepper and roast for 20–25 minutes, until tender and golden in places. Repeat with the broccoli and remaining oil, rubbing the oil well into the florets with your hands. Season and roast for 15–20 minutes. Turn the squash, seeds and broccoli halfway through cooking so they brown evenly.

Meanwhile, make the smashed beans. Heat 4 tablespoons of the oil over a medium-low heat, add the garlic and cook for 1 minute, stirring. Add the beans, lemon zest, juice and stock and cook for 5 minutes, crushing the beans with the end of a wooden spoon to break them up. Add more stock if they seem dry and powdery – you want it to be a bit saucy. Season with salt and pepper, to taste.

Spoon the beans onto 4 serving plates and top with the roasted broccoli and squash. Scatter the feta, dukkah and roasted squash seeds over and drizzle with the remaining oil. Squeeze over a little extra lemon juice, if liked.

Smoked chilli butter greens with tagliatelle

Flavoured butters are perfect for the flexitarian kitchen... the options are plentiful and a dish can readily be adapted to suit varying tastes, vegetarian or not. It pays to double the recipe and any leftover butter can be rolled in cling film/plastic wrap into a cylinder and stored in the freezer. When you want to use it, simply slice into rounds. This smoky, chilli-hot buttery pasta dish also features generous amounts of winter veg, including greens, leeks and broccoli, but do substitute according to your taste and what you have to hand.

Serves **4**
Preparation time: **20 minutes,** plus optional soaking time
Cooking time: **14 minutes**

400g/14oz dried tagliatelle pasta
2 leeks, quartered lengthways and thinly sliced
400g/14oz greens or Savoy cabbage, shredded
200g/7oz broccoli florets
salt and freshly ground black pepper
squeeze of lemon juice, to serve
dried chilli/hot pepper flakes and vegetarian Parmesan, to serve (optional)

Smoked chilli butter
2 dried chipotle chillies or 1 tbsp chipotle chilli powder
4 garlic cloves
juice of ½ lemon
100g/3½oz/scant ½ cup butter or dairy-free alternative

First, make the smoked chilli butter. Soak the dried chillies in just-boiled water for 20 minutes or until softened. Deseed the chillies, then blitz in a mini food processor or blender with the rest of the flavoured butter ingredients. (If using chipotle powder, there is no need to soak.) Season, then spoon into a dish and chill until needed.

Cook the tagliatelle in plenty of boiling salted water following the package directions. Drain the pasta, reserving 200ml/7fl oz/scant 1 cup of the cooking water.

Meanwhile, cook the cabbage in boiling salted water for 2–3 minutes or until just tender. Drain and refresh under cold running water.

Steam the leeks for 3–4 minutes, then refresh as above. Finally, steam the broccoli for 4–5 minutes, then refresh.

Return the cooked pasta to the pan, add the vegetables and the smoked chilli butter, and warm through for 2 minutes, adding enough of the pasta cooking water to loosen, turning the pasta and vegetables until combined and coated in the buttery juices. Season, add a good squeeze of lemon juice, and serve with dried chilli/hot pepper flakes and grated Parmesan, if you like.

PART-TIME VARIATIONS

Smoky bacon butter Replace the chipotle chillies with 4 rashers nitrate-free smoked bacon. Grill/broil the bacon until crisp, then break into small pieces and blend with the rest of the ingredients.

Anchovy butter Replace the chipotle chillies with 8 anchovy fillets in oil, drained, then blend with the rest of the ingredients.

Seaweed butter Replace the chipotle chillies with 2 tbsp dried nori or dulse flakes (you can blitz the seaweed into a powder, but I like a bit of texture), then blend with the rest of the ingredients.

Mushroom noodle larb

~~~~~~~~~~~~~~~~~~~~~~~~~~~~~~~~

Sizzling woks of larb are a familiar sight in the vibrant street food markets of Bangkok. Traditionally a stir-fried minced/ground pork salad, chopped mushrooms, or indeed aubergine/eggplant, make perfect meat-free alternatives. For a more substantial meal, this has the addition of noodles. As with all Thai food, the balance of tastes and textures is vital, so there are 4 key flavours – salty, spicy, sour and sweet – and a mixture of soft and crunchy ingredients.

Serves **4**
Preparation time: **15 minutes**
Cooking time: **15 minutes**

2 tbsp sunflower oil

500g/1lb 2oz chestnut/cremini mushrooms, finely chopped

3 banana shallots, thinly sliced

4 spring onions/scallions, sliced diagonally

1 red pepper, deseeded and diced

3 lemongrass stalks, peeled and finely chopped

1 thumb-size piece of fresh root ginger, finely chopped

4 garlic cloves, finely chopped

4 kaffir lime leaves, shredded

1 red bird's eye chilli, deseeded and thinly sliced

600g/1lb 5oz cooked medium noodles

juice of 1 lime, plus extra wedges

2 tbsp light soy sauce

1–2 tsp soft light brown sugar

3 large handfuls of chopped fresh coriander/cilantro leaves

2 large handfuls of chopped fresh mint leaves

sea salt and freshly ground black pepper

To serve

1 Little Gem/Bibb lettuce, leaves separated

70g/2½oz/¾ cup chopped roasted unsalted peanuts

Heat a large dry wok or frying pan over a high heat. When hot, add the oil and mushrooms and stir-fry for 8 minutes until they start to turn golden – you want to cook off any liquid from the mushrooms.

Add a splash more oil, followed by the shallots, the white parts of the spring onions/scallions, red pepper, lemongrass, ginger, garlic, lime leaves and half of the chilli, and stir-fry for another 2 minutes.

Add the noodles to the wok, loosening them with your hands. Turn the heat down to medium-low, add the lime juice, soy sauce, sugar and half the coriander/cilantro and mint. Using tongs, turn until everything is combined and heated through. Remove from the heat and season with salt and pepper, to taste, bearing in mind the soy is pretty salty. Taste and adjust flavourings, if needed.

Arrange the lettuce leaves in 4 large, shallow serving bowls and top with the mushroom noodles. Scatter over the reserved green parts of the spring onions/scallions, the rest of the herbs and the peanuts, before serving with extra wedges of lime.

· ·

PART-TIME VARIATIONS

Pork noodle larb Swap half the mushrooms for 250g/9oz minced/ground pork and stir-fry for 10 minutes before continuing as above. Swap 1 tbsp of the soy sauce for 1 tbsp fish sauce.

Mushroom larb wraps with pickled turnip For a light meal, leave out the noodles and serve the mushroom larb spooned into the hollows of Little Gem/Bibb lettuce leaves and topped with a turnip pickle. To make the pickle, mix together 2 tbsp caster/superfine sugar, ½ tsp sea salt and 2 tbsp rice vinegar with 2 tbsp warm water in a bowl. Stir in 125g/4½oz turnip and 1 small raw beetroot/beet, both peeled and cut into thin matchsticks.

Beetroot spaghetti
with goat's cheese and walnuts

Nutritionally speaking, wholewheat pasta beats white pasta hands down, yet its 'brownness', albeit fitting with the season, could be described as a bit lack-lustre. To brighten things up, cooked fresh beetroot/beet is used here to add both colour and flavour to the pasta in this quick and easy meal.

Serves **4**
Preparation time: **10 minutes**
Cooking time: **15 minutes**

400g/14oz dried wholewheat spaghetti
200g/7oz cooked beetroot/beet in natural juice (not vinegar), drained and roughly chopped
75g/2½oz/½ cup walnut pieces
2 tbsp extra virgin olive oil, plus extra for drizzling
2 garlic cloves, finely chopped
100g/3½oz rindless soft goat's cheese, crumbled or dairy-free alternative
4 handfuls of rocket/arugula leaves
sea salt and freshly ground black pepper

Cook the spaghetti in plenty of boiling salted water following the package directions. While the pasta is cooking, purée the beetroot/beet using a hand-held stick/immersion blender and set aside.

Toast the walnuts in a large, dry frying pan for 3 minutes, tossing them occasionally until they start to colour. Set aside.

Heat the oil in a large sauté pan over a medium heat. Fry the garlic for 1 minute, then add the beetroot/beet purée and cook, stirring, for 2 minutes until reduced slightly.

When the pasta is cooked but still al dente, drain, reserving 100ml/3½fl oz/scant ½ cup of the cooking water. Add the pasta to the beetroot/beet along with enough of the cooking water to loosen the sauce. Using tongs, turn the pasta to coat it in the sauce, adding more of the cooking water if needed.

Divide the pasta between 4 large shallow bowls and scatter over the toasted walnuts and goat's cheese just before serving. Top with the rocket/arugula and an extra drizzle of olive oil, then season with salt and pepper, to taste.

. . . .
PART-TIME VARIATION

Beetroot spaghetti with steak and walnuts Swap the goat's cheese and walnuts for 2 sirloin steaks. Season the steaks and drizzle with olive oil, then sear them briefly in a hot frying pan for 2–3 minutes, or until cooked to your liking, turning once. Leave to rest for 5 minutes, then cut into thin slices. Serve on top of the pasta with shavings of Parmesan and a good handful of rocket/arugula leaves.

Baked cauliflower cheese risotto

〰️〰️〰️〰️〰️〰️〰️〰️〰️〰️〰️〰️〰️〰️〰️〰️〰️〰️

Pure comfort food... this creamy cheesy risotto uses cauliflower in three ways, which really goes to show the versatility of one humble vegetable. It's grated into rice-like grains and mixed into the Arborio rice; roasted in florets to grace the top of the risotto; and finally the leaves are roasted to serve as a side. What's more, the risotto is cooked in the oven, so you don't have to spend time stirring it on the hob. Just bung it in the oven and leave it to do its own thing. Although don't let me stop you if you want to make the risotto in the traditional way – there are definitely times when stirring a pot over the stove can be therapeutic!

Serves **4**
Preparation time: **20 minutes**
Cooking time: **40 minutes**

250g/9oz cauliflower, with inner leaves still attached
2 tbsp olive oil, plus extra for drizzling
2 onions, finely chopped
3 garlic cloves, finely chopped
325g/11½oz/1¾ cups Arborio rice, rinsed
185ml/6fl oz/¾ cup dry white wine
1 litre/35fl oz/4¼ cups hot vegetable stock
4 tsp fresh thyme leaves or 2 tsp dried
1 tsp smoked paprika
1½ tbsp unsalted butter
80g/2¾oz/1¼ cups vegetarian Parmesan cheese, finely grated
50g/1¾oz/½ cup walnut halves
sea salt and freshly ground black pepper

Coarsely grate half of the cauliflower, including the stalk. Break the remaining cauliflower into florets and set aside with the inner leaves.

Preheat the oven to 180°C/350°F/Gas 4.

Heat 1 tablespoon of the oil in a large ovenproof saucepan over a medium-low heat, add the onions and cook, covered, for 8 minutes, until softened but not coloured. Stir in the garlic and cook for another 1 minute. Add the rice and grated cauliflower, stir to coat in the onion mixture and cook for 2 minutes, stirring continuously to stop anything sticking. Pour in the wine and cook over a medium heat, stirring, until the wine is absorbed and there is no smell of alcohol. Pour in the stock and add the thyme, stir well, then cover with a lid. Put the pan in the oven for 20–25 minutes, stirring halfway.

Meanwhile, mix together the remaining oil and paprika in a mixing bowl and season with salt and pepper. Add the cauliflower florets and turn to coat them in the paprika oil, then tip them onto a large baking sheet and roast for 20–25 minutes, turning once, until golden and tender. After 10 minutes, drizzle a little oil over the cauliflower leaves and add them to the baking sheet with the florets.

The walnuts can be toasted at the same time. Arrange them on a separate baking sheet and toast in the oven for 12–15 minutes until slightly golden. Remove from the oven and roughly chop.

The rice is ready when tender but still slightly al dente at the core and all the stock has been absorbed. Remove the pan from the oven, gently stir in the butter and three-quarters of the Parmesan and check the seasoning, adding salt and pepper, to taste. Leave to stand, covered, for 5 minutes.

To serve, spoon the risotto into large, shallow bowls, then top with the cauliflower florets and the remaining Parmesan. Scatter over the walnuts and arrange the cauliflower leaves by the side.

PART-TIME VARIATIONS

Baked cauliflower cheese risotto with Parma ham In place of the toasted walnuts, opt for 4 slices of Parma ham. Place the Parma ham in the oven on a lined baking sheet at the same time as the risotto for 5–10 minutes, turning once, until crisp. Serve on top of the risotto with the cauliflower florets and leaves and a sprinkling of Parmesan.

Vegan baked cauliflower 'cheese' risotto Use non-dairy spread instead of the butter and stir in 4 tbsp nutritional yeast flakes in place of the Parmesan. To add a creaminess, stir in 3 tbsp vegan cream cheese at the end of the cooking time.

Baked cauliflower cheese risotto with smoked trout Instead of the walnuts, top the cauliflower-cheese risotto with 2 cooked hot-smoked trout fillets, skin removed and flesh flaked. Alternatively, try 100g/3½oz cold-smoked trout, cut into strips as a topping.

Meal for a gathering

MENU
Serves 4 (6 at a stretch)

○○

Pot-roasted cauliflower in cider with apples

○○

Scandi-style potato gratin

○○

Rainbow chard with lemon butter

This really is a meal for hunkering down to enjoy with friends and family. Pure comfort food, this harvest festival of autumn/fall vegetables is enlivened with warming spices, cider, apples, herbs, nuts and seeds. While cauliflower is pretty much available all year round, it is at its peak in early autumn/fall. Look for a large one encased in unwilted green leaves, as this is a good indication that the florets are in the best condition, too. It makes a stunning centrepiece surrounded by the cider-imbued apples and onions and topped with a savoury granola. The lightly spiced potato gratin with its creamy sauce makes the perfect accompaniment. For a touch of colour, there's rainbow chard with its vibrant pink, yellow and white stalks.

Pot-roasted cauliflower in cider with apples

Preparation time: 20 minutes | Cooking time: 1 hour 10 minutes

1 large cauliflower, about 950g/2lb 2oz, outer leaves removed; pale green inner leaves reserved

1½ tbsp extra virgin olive oil

2 onions, trimmed, halved and each cut into 8 wedges

3 garlic cloves, thinly sliced

2 tsp fresh thyme leaves or 1 tsp dried thyme

200ml/7fl oz/scant 1 cup dry cider, plus extra if needed

2 apples, skin on, halved, cored and each cut into 6 wedges

3 tbsp nonpareil capers, drained and patted dry

25g/1oz/2 tbsp butter or dairy-free spread

sea salt and freshly ground black pepper

Savoury granola

4 tbsp jumbo porridge/rolled oats

40g/1½oz/⅓ cup blanched hazelnuts

40g/1½oz/⅓ cup pumpkin seeds

40g/1½oz/⅓ cup sunflower seeds

Preheat the oven to 220°C/425°F/Gas 7.

To prepare the cauliflower, trim the thick central stalk without cutting into the florets, then make a deep cross-shaped cut into the stalk.

Heat 1 tablespoon oil in a large, heavy-based casserole dish/Dutch oven with a lid, over a medium heat. Add the onions and cook for 5 minutes, stirring occasionally, until softened but not coloured. Add the garlic and thyme and cook for 1 minute, then pour in the cider and let it bubble away until reduced by half and there is no aroma of alcohol, about 4 minutes. Season with salt and pepper. Remove the pan from the heat, sit the cauliflower on top of the onions and spoon some of the pan juices over the top to moisten it. Tuck the apples around the cauliflower, spooning over the pan juices, cover with the lid and roast for 40 minutes. From time to time, check that the pan hasn't dried out and add a splash more cider, if needed.

Meanwhile, make the granola. Toast the oats in a large, dry frying pan over a medium-low heat for 5 minutes, turning occasionally, until they start to turn golden. Tip into a bowl and repeat with the hazelnuts and seeds, toasting for 3–5 minutes each or until light golden. Tip into the bowl with the oats, stir, season, and leave to cool.

Heat the remaining oil in the frying pan over a medium heat, add the capers and cook, stirring, for 3 minutes, or until crisp (take care as they can spit). Remove with a slotted spoon to drain on paper towels.

Remove the lid from the dish, smear the butter or spread all over the cauliflower and return it to the oven for 20 minutes or until the cauliflower is tender to the point of a skewer and golden on top. Place it on a serving plate, spoon the onions and apples around, and spoon over the juices from the pan. Check the seasoning and add more salt and pepper, if needed, then scatter over the capers and some of the granola mix; the rest can be placed in a bowl on the table to let everyone help themselves.

Scandi-style potato gratin

Preparation time: 15 minutes | Cooking time: 1 hour

600ml/21fl oz/2½ cups good-quality hot
  vegetable stock
6 heaped tbsp thick double/heavy cream
  or dairy-free alternative
2 tsp Dijon mustard
1 tsp ground allspice
½ tsp ground cloves
900g/2lb white potatoes, such as Maris
  Piper, skin on, scrubbed
1 large onion, very thinly sliced
4 bay leaves
25g/1oz/2 tbsp butter or dairy-free spread,
  plus extra for greasing
sea salt and freshly ground black pepper

Preheat the oven to 220°C/425°F/Gas
7. Mix together the hot stock, cream,
mustard and spices in a jug. Season
generously with salt and pepper, then
set aside.

Using a mandoline or vegetable slicer,
cut the potatoes into thin matchsticks.
Tip them into a bowl of cold water as you
go to stop them discolouring. Drain the
potatoes well and pat dry with a clean
kitchen cloth.

Layer the potatoes and onion in a large,
greased ovenproof dish. Pour the stock
mixture over, tucking in the bay leaves,
cover with foil and bake for 40 minutes.
Remove the foil, dot the butter or spread
over the top and return to the oven for
another 20 minutes or until the potatoes
are tender and the top is crisp.

· ·

PART-TIME VARIATION

Scandi-style potato gratin with anchovies or smoked mackerel Stir 5 drained and
chopped anchovies in oil into the creamy sauce mixture. Alternatively, flake 1 fillet
skinless smoked mackerel into small pieces and add to the potato and onion mixture
before adding the sauce.

Rainbow chard with lemon butter

Preparation time: 5 minutes | Cooking time: 10 minutes

400g/14oz rainbow chard, stalks and
    leaves separated, sliced
sea salt and freshly ground black pepper

Lemon butter
40g/1½oz/2½ tbsp butter or dairy-free
    spread
finely grated zest of ½ unwaxed lemon
    and juice of 1

Steam the chard stalks for 2–3 minutes
or until tender, refresh under cold
running water, then tip into a bowl. Steam
the leaves – you may need to do this in
2–3 batches – for 2 minutes or until just
tender and wilted, then refresh under
cold running water. Drain the stalks
and leaves well, squeezing out any
excess water.

Heat the butter or spread in a large sauté
pan over a medium heat. When melted,
add the lemon zest and juice, tip in the
chard and turn to coat it in the lemony
butter. Warm through briefly and season
with salt and pepper, to taste.

Smoky aubergine chilli

You can't beat a good vegetarian chilli and this one certainly packs a punch with a delicious smoky heat from the dried chipotle chillies. I've used aduki beans instead of the more usual kidney beans, as I prefer their smaller size, but do go for whichever type of bean that works for you. Serve with rice, sour cream, slices of avocado and a final sprinkling of coriander/cilantro.

Serves **4–6**
Preparation time: **20 minutes,**
plus soaking
Cooking time: **1 hour 35 minutes**

150g/5½oz/generous ¾ cup dried aduki beans, soaked overnight (or 300g/10½oz/1½ cups canned aduki beans, drained and rinsed)
500g/1lb 2oz sweet potatoes or butternut squash, peeled and cut into bite-size chunks
3 tbsp olive oil
2 large onions, roughly chopped
1 aubergine/eggplant, cut into small dice
4 garlic cloves, finely chopped
1 red pepper, deseeded and chopped
2 tsp dried chipotle chilli flakes
1 tsp cumin seeds
2 tsp mild smoked paprika
1 tsp ground coriander
1 tsp ground allspice
400g/14oz can chopped tomatoes
1 tsp vegetable bouillon powder
2 tsp liquid smoke or vegetarian Worcestershire sauce
3 tbsp tomato purée/paste
1 tsp soft light brown sugar
sea salt and freshly ground black pepper

Drain the soaked dried beans, put them in a saucepan and generously cover with cold water. Bring to the boil and cook for 10 minutes, then reduce the heat slightly, part-cover with a lid and simmer for 1¼ hours, or until tender.

While the beans are cooking, preheat the oven to 200°C/400°F/Gas 6. Toss the sweet potatoes or squash in 1 tablespoon of the oil and spread out a large baking sheet. Roast for 30 minutes, turning once, until cooked and golden in places.

Heat the remaining oil in a large saucepan over a medium heat and fry the onions for 5 minutes. Add the aubergine/eggplant, garlic and red pepper and cook for another 5 minutes, stirring, until softened – you may need to add a splash more oil. Stir in the spices, followed by the chopped tomatoes, 500ml/17fl oz/2 cups water, the bouillon powder, liquid smoke or Worcestershire sauce, tomato purée/paste and sugar. Stir well until combined, bring almost to the boil, then reduce the heat and simmer, part-covered, for 20 minutes.

Stir in the roasted sweet potato or squash and cooked aduki beans and simmer for another 20 minutes – leave the lid off if the sauce needs to reduce down or add a splash more water, if needed. Season with salt and pepper, to taste. Serve the chilli with rice, soured cream, avocado and a scattering of coriander.

PART-TIME VARIATION

Chilli with beef Try swapping the aubergine/eggplant for 250g/9oz minced/ground beef. Brown the meat in a splash of olive oil for 5 minutes before adding the onion and carrying on with the rest of the recipe, as above, or until the beef is tender.

Sri Lankan-style jackfruit curry
with rainbow chard

〜〜〜〜〜〜〜〜〜〜〜〜〜〜〜〜〜〜〜〜〜

This brings back memories of a visit to a spice garden on the magical island of Sri Lanka. The lush garden was fragrant with cinnamon, mace, nutmeg, pepper and cardamom. Spices, jackfruit and coconut are synonymous with Sri Lanka and all are used in this creamy, aromatic curry. I can't say the same for chard, but it's in season in autumn/fall and the rainbow variety with its glam pink and yellow stalks brighten up any dish. I also like to make this curry with squash or pumpkin instead of the jackfruit – carrot and swede/rutabaga would be good, too, at this time of year.

Serves **4**
Preparation time: **25 minutes**
Cooking time: **25 minutes**

3 tbsp coconut or sunflower oil
2 onions, chopped
4 garlic cloves, finely chopped
2 green chillies, finely chopped
400g/14oz can coconut milk
400ml/14fl oz/1⅔ cups good-quality vegetable stock
2 tsp ground turmeric
½ cinnamon stick
250g/9oz canned jackfruit, drained, core discarded and torn into pieces
125g/4½oz rainbow chard, leaves and stalks separated, both thinly sliced
finely grated zest and juice of 1 unwaxed lime
sea salt and freshly ground black pepper
brown basmati rice, to serve

Spice blend

½ tsp fenugreek seeds
1 tsp coriander seeds
6 cardamom pods, seeds removed
5 cloves
½ tsp black mustard seeds
5 curry leaves
½ tsp dried chilli/hot pepper flakes

Heat 2 tablespoons of the oil in a saucepan over a medium heat, add the onions and cook for 8 minutes, part-covered with a lid and stirring occasionally, until softened but not coloured. Add the garlic and chillies and cook for another 2 minutes. Pour in the coconut milk and stock. Add the turmeric and cinnamon stick, stir, and simmer over a medium-low heat for 10 minutes. Add the jackfruit and chard leaves and simmer, covered, for another 5 minutes.

Meanwhile, grind the fenugreek, coriander and cardamom seeds and cloves in a spice grinder or using a pestle and mortar. Heat the remaining 1 tablespoon of oil in a frying pan, add the ground spices, mustard seeds, curry leaves, dried chilli/hot pepper flakes along with the chard stalks and fry for 1–2 minutes or until the stalks are tender.

Remove the cinnamon stick from the curry and stir in the spice mix and chard stalks. Add the lime zest and juice, then season with salt and pepper. Serve with rice.

· ·
PART-TIME VARIATION

Sri Lankan chicken curry with rainbow chard Replace the jackfruit with 250g/9oz cubed chicken breasts. Add to the pan at the same time as you would the jackfruit and cook for 5 minutes as instructed above.

Beetroot tarts with goat's cheese and dukkah

I make no apology for including two recipes using beetroot and goat's cheese in this book – the deep purple of beetroot brings a touch of colour and a delicious earthy note, making it a natural partner to the goat's cheese, horseradish and spices in these tarts.

Makes **6**
Preparation time: **15 minutes**
Cooking time: **50 minutes**

4 smallish raw beetroot/beets, about 270g/9½oz total weight
2 tbsp apple cider vinegar
3 tbsp crème fraîche
3 tbsp hot horseradish sauce
1 x 320g/11¼oz pack ready-rolled, all-butter puff pastry
1 egg, lightly beaten
1 tbsp runny honey
75g/2½oz soft rindless goat's cheese, crumbled

Dukkah
1 tbsp coriander seeds
1 tsp cumin seeds
2 tbsp pumpkin seeds
1½ tbsp sesame seeds
50g/1¾oz/⅓ cup blanched hazelnuts
¼–½ tsp dried chilli/hot pepper flakes
sea salt and freshly ground black pepper

Put the beetroot/beets in a pan with enough hot water to cover, add the vinegar and bring to the boil. Cook for 15–20 minutes until tender to the point of a skewer. Drain and leave until cool enough to handle. Rub off the skins and slice into fairly thin rounds.

Meanwhile, preheat the oven to 220°C/425°F/Gas 7 and line 2 baking sheets with baking paper. Mix together the crème fraîche and horseradish sauce and set aside.

Cut the pastry sheet into 6 rectangles. Score a border, 1cm/½in from the edge, around each and prick the bases with a fork. Arrange on the baking sheets and chill until the beetroot/beets are ready.

To assemble the tarts, spoon the crème fraîche mixture on top of each pastry base, keeping within the border. Arrange the beetroot slices on top, slightly overlapping and dab with a little oil. Brush the pastry edges with beaten egg (avoid touching the beetroot). Bake for 25 minutes, then brush the beetroot with honey and bake for another 5 minutes until the pastry is golden.

Meanwhile, make the dukkah. Toast the coriander and cumin seeds in a dry frying pan for 2 minutes, tossing occasionally, until aromatic. Leave to cool. Repeat with the pumpkin seeds, sesame seeds and hazelnuts, toasting them for 3–5 minutes until slightly coloured. Place the spices, seeds and nuts in a mini food processor and pulse until coarsely chopped. Stir in the chilli flakes, and season.

Just before serving, crumble the goat's cheese over each tart and top with a spoonful of dukkah – they are best served warm.

· ·
PART-TIME VARIATIONS

Cashew cream cheese and beetroot tarts Swap the crème fraîche and horseradish mixture for Cashew Cream Cheese (see page 94) and use maple syrup instead of honey for brushing.

Smoked salmon and beetroot tarts with dill Swap the dukkah and goat's cheese for 150g/5½oz smoked salmon. When the tarts are cooked, drape a few slices of salmon over each, add a squeeze of lemon juice, season with black pepper, and finish with dill sprigs.

Pho with greens and pickled turnip

〰〰〰〰〰〰〰〰〰〰〰〰〰〰〰〰

Turnips are much under-rated and are just as nice eaten raw as they are cooked. With their good crunch and slightly radishy flavour, they make a great pickle (see page 131) to serve with this version of the iconic Vietnamese noodle broth, *pho*. Packed with flavour and goodness, you could make the broth up to 2 days in advance to allow the spices to infuse. Keep it in the refrigerator, then strain before continuing with the rest of the recipe. Fried marinated tempeh, tofu or egg could be added to the list of serving suggestions.

Serves **4**
Preparation time: **20 minutes**, plus infusing
Cooking time: **35 minutes**

3 star anise

8 cloves

½ cinnamon stick

1 tsp coriander seeds

1 onion, peeled and cut into 6 wedges

15g/½oz dried Chinese mushrooms

5cm/2in piece of fresh root ginger, cut into thin rounds

1.5 litres/52fl oz/6½ cups good-quality vegetable stock

2 tbsp light soy sauce

150g/5½oz broccoli, cut into small florets, stalks cut into matchsticks

125g/4½oz Savoy cabbage or kale, shredded

200g/7oz flat rice noodles

juice of 1 lime, or more to taste

freshly ground black pepper

To serve

2 spring onions/scallions, thinly sliced diagonally

1 handful of Thai basil or regular basil leaves

1 red bird's eye chilli, deseeded and finely chopped

1 tsp toasted sesame seeds

Pickled Turnip (see page 131)

lime wedges

sriracha chilli sauce (optional)

To start the broth, put the star anise, cloves, cinnamon stick and coriander seeds in a dry frying pan and toast over a medium-low heat for 1–2 minutes, tossing occasionally, until fragrant, then tip into a large saucepan. Put the onion in the hot, dry frying pan and char for 5 minutes, turning occasionally, until blackened in places. Add to the pan with the aromatics, dried mushrooms, ginger, stock and soy sauce. Bring almost to the boil, then reduce the heat to low and simmer, covered, for 30 minutes. Turn off the heat and leave the broth to infuse for 30 minutes, or longer if you have time.

Meanwhile, steam the broccoli for 5 minutes, then the cabbage for 2 minutes until just tender. Refresh under cold water and set aside.

Cook the noodles following the package directions, then drain and refresh. Set aside.

When the broth has infused, strain, then pick out the dried mushrooms and thinly slice. Discard the aromatics and onion. Pour the broth back into the pan and add the sliced mushrooms, green vegetables and lime juice and reheat briefly. Taste and adjust the seasoning, adding more soy sauce and lime juice as needed.

Pour just-boiled water from a kettle over the noodles to reheat, then divide between 4 large, shallow bowls. Ladle over the broth and vegetables. Top with the spring onions/scallions, herbs, chilli and sesame seeds. Serve with the pickled turnip, with wedges of lime and a dash of sriracha, if you like it hot.

· ·

PART-TIME VARIATIONS

Leftover roast meats Top with roast meat, such as beef, chicken or pork, cut into thin strips and stir-fried in sesame oil and soy sauce for 3 minutes. If you have a chicken carcass you could make a stock with water, onion, bay leaves, carrot, celery and black peppercorns.

Polenta bowl with cavolo nero and chestnut crumbs

A hug in a bowl... Cavolo nero, a dark-leaved type of kale with an Italian heritage, is perfect stir-fried as the leaves are sturdy enough to keep their texture when cooked without wilting to insignificance. Their robust texture is important in this dish as it's the perfect foil to the smooth polenta/cornmeal and crisp chestnut crumbs.

Serves **4**
Preparation time: **20 minutes**
Cooking time: **20 minutes**

1.3 litres/46fl oz/5½ cups good-quality hot vegetable stock
250g/9oz/1⅔ cups instant fine polenta/cornmeal
75g/2½oz/scant 1 cup vegetarian Parmesan, finely grated
25g/1oz/2 tbsp butter
1 tbsp olive oil
300g/10½oz cavolo nero, central stems removed and leaves torn into pieces
2 garlic cloves, finely chopped
finely grated zest and juice of 1 unwaxed lemon
sea salt and freshly ground black pepper

Chestnut crumbs
1 tbsp olive oil
250g/9oz/1¾ cups cooked chestnuts, roughly chopped
2 tsp finely chopped fresh rosemary
1½ tsp fresh thyme leaves or ¾ tsp dried
1 medium-hot red chilli, deseeded and finely chopped

To make the chestnut crumbs, heat the olive oil in a large frying pan over a medium heat, add the chestnuts and cook for 8 minutes or until they start to crisp up and turn golden. Stir in the herbs and chilli, then season with salt and pepper. Tip into a bowl and keep warm in a low oven.

Meanwhile, bring the stock to a rolling boil in a saucepan. Gradually pour in the polenta/cornmeal, stirring continuously with a balloon whisk to stop lumps forming. Cook, now stirring with a wooden spoon, for about 8–10 minutes until smooth – it shouldn't taste grainy at this point. I prefer a slightly loose mixture, slightly runnier than mashed potatoes, so add more hot stock or water if needed. When you feel it is ready, stir in the Parmesan and butter and season with salt and pepper, to taste. Cover with a lid and leave to sit briefly while you cook the cavolo nero.

Heat the olive oil in a large frying pan over a medium heat. Add the cavolo nero; it may look too much for the pan, but will soon wilt down. Sauté for 2 minutes, turning the leaves with tongs so it cooks evenly. Add the garlic and cook for another 1 minute. Add the lemon zest and juice and season with salt and pepper.

Spoon the polenta/cornmeal into 4 large shallow bowls, top with the cavolo nero and scatter over the chestnut crumbs.

· ·
PART-TIME VARIATION

Polenta bowl with cavolo nero and crispy pork topping Mix 250g/9oz minced/ground pork with ¼ tsp grated nutmeg, 1½ tsp fresh thyme leaves (or ¾ tsp dried), 2 finely chopped garlic cloves and 2 tsp finely chopped rosemary. Season with salt and pepper. Heat 1 tbsp olive oil in a large frying pan over a medium heat, add the pork mixture and cook for 10 minutes or until the meat turns slightly crisp and golden. Serve on top of the polenta/cornmeal with the cavolo nero.

Autumn kale Caesar salad

Serves **4**
Preparation time: **15 minutes**
Cooking time: **5 minutes**

Purists may wince at this twist on the classic Caesar salad, made with kale rather the more usual romaine lettuce, yet the classic creamy Parmesan dressing – without the usual anchovies – is equally delicious with this mix of green leaves, red cabbage, chickpeas/garbanzo beans and red onion. And the croutons add a lovely garlicky crunch. For a more substantial salad, top each serving with a soft-boiled egg, or flexitarians may like a chargrilled chicken breast, cut into strips.

4 slices ciabatta bread, torn into chunks
1 large garlic clove, peeled, left whole and cut in half lengthways
extra-virgin olive oil, for drizzling
100g/3½oz kale, tough stalks removed, leaves torn if large
125g/4½oz red cabbage, shredded
½ small red onion, thinly sliced
100g/3½oz/¾ cup drained canned chickpeas/garbanzo beans
2 tbsp pumpkin seeds, toasted

Dressing
2 egg yolks
8 tbsp olive oil
2 garlic cloves, crushed
juice of 1 lemon
40g/1½oz/⅔ cup vegetarian Parmesan cheese, finely grated
sea salt and freshly ground black pepper

Preheat the grill/broiler to high. Toast the bread on both sides until golden. Rub the cut-side of the garlic over the top of each slice and drizzle oil over both sides. Tear the toasted bread into bite-size chunks. Set aside.

To make the dressing, put the egg yolks in a mixing bowl and slowly pour in the oil, whisking continuously, until you reach the consistency of mayonnaise. Whisk in the garlic and lemon juice, followed by the Parmesan. Season with salt and pepper, to taste.

Put the kale in a serving bowl, add 4 tablespoons of the dressing and rub it into the kale until the leaves begin to soften and are coated. Top the kale with the red cabbage, onion and chickpeas/garbanzo beans, then drizzle over as much dressing as you like and finish with the croutons and pumpkin seeds.

. . . .
PART-TIME VARIATIONS

Anchovy dressing For a more traditional dressing, mash 2 drained sliced anchovies in oil into the egg yolk, then continue with the method, as above.

Dairy-free cashew dressing Soak 55g/2oz/½ cup cashew nuts in warm water for 1 hour. Drain, then tip into a blender with 4 tbsp olive oil, 1 crushed garlic clove, 2 tbsp nutritional yeast flakes and the juice of ½ lemon. Add 2 tbsp water and blend until smooth and creamy. Season with salt and pepper, then taste, adding more water or lemon juice to make a smooth, runny dressing.

Roasted carrot and couscous salad
with chimichurri

Who said couscous salads were uninteresting? If you're lucky enough to have the green tops on your carrots, don't waste them as they can be turned into this chimichurri sauce. Don't worry if your carrots don't come with their tops; opt for flat-leaf parsley instead. And if you can find rainbow carrots, which come in yellow, orange and purple, then all the better.

Serves **4**
Preparation time: **20 minutes**
Cooking time: **30 minutes**

2 tsp harissa paste
juice of 1 lemon
2 tbsp extra virgin olive oil
6 carrots, scrubbed and green tops saved (see below)
150g/5½oz/scant 1 cup whole-wheat couscous
½ tsp ground turmeric
3 handfuls of fresh flat-leaf parsley, chopped
2 handfuls of fresh mint leaves, chopped
55g/2oz/⅓ cup roasted almonds, preferably smoked, chopped
sea salt and freshly ground black pepper

Dressing
3 tbsp extra virgin olive oil
finely grated zest and juice of 1 large unwaxed lemon
¼ tsp allspice

Chimichurri (optional)
1 handful of carrot tops (see above) or flat-leaf parsley
1 handful of basil leaves
1 red jalapeño chilli, deseeded
1 garlic clove, peeled
1 tbsp white wine vinegar
5 tbsp extra virgin olive oil
a squeeze of lemon juice (optional)

Preheat the oven to 200°C/400°F/Gas 6.

Mix together the harissa, lemon juice and olive oil in a mixing bowl. Season with salt and pepper. Cut 5 of the carrots into long batons, add to the bowl, then turn to coat them in the marinade. Tip onto a baking sheet, spread out evenly and roast for 25–30 minutes until tender and starting to colour.

Meanwhile, put the couscous and turmeric into a large bowl, pour over 200ml/7fl oz/scant 1 cup just-boiled water. Season, stir until combined, then cover with a plate and leave to stand for 5 minutes, or until the water has been absorbed and the couscous is cooked.

Mix together all the ingredients for the dressing, seasoning to taste.

If making the chimichurri sauce, put all the ingredients in a small food processor or blender and pulse briefly until roughly chopped – take care as you don't want it to be too smooth. Taste, season and add lemon juice, if needed.

Finely grate the remaining carrot and stir it into the cooked couscous with most of the parsley and mint, leaving a small amount of the herbs to garnish. Pour the dressing over the couscous and turn it gently until mixed together. Top the couscous with the reserved herbs, roasted carrots and almonds. Serve with a spoonful of the chimichurri sauce, if using.

Autumn squash pilaf
with spinach yogurt sauce

〰〰〰〰〰〰〰〰〰〰〰〰〰〰〰〰〰〰〰〰

Serves **4**
Preparation time: **20 minutes**
Cooking time: **30 minutes**

Autumn/fall is squash time. I've suggested butternut squash as it's readily available, but look out for other types, such as acorn, crown prince or kabocha. This simple pilaf is flavoured with baharat, a Middle Eastern spice blend that has a distinctive smoky, sweet flavour. It is easy to make your own, but can also be found in large supermarkets and Middle Eastern grocers.

800g/1lb 12oz butternut squash, peeled, deseeded and cut into large bite-size chunks (550g/1lb 4oz prepped weight)

3 tbsp olive oil

250g/9oz baby spinach

150g/5½oz/scant ¾ cup Greek-style yogurt or dairy-free alternative

5 garlic cloves, minced

juice of 1½ lemons, plus finely grated zest of 1 unwaxed lemon

1 litre/35fl oz/4¼ cups good-quality hot vegetable stock

250g/9oz/1½ cups bulgur wheat, rinsed

1 tsp ground turmeric

2 onions, finely chopped

1 heaped tbsp baharat spice mix

20g/¾oz/4 tsp butter or dairy-free equivalent

1 large handful of fresh mint leaves, roughly chopped

sea salt and freshly ground black pepper

Preheat the oven to 200°C/400°F/Gas 6. Place the squash on a large baking sheet, drizzle over 1 tablespoon of the oil and turn until well coated. Roast for 25–30 minutes, turning halfway, until tender.

Meanwhile, make the sauce. Steam 75g/2½oz of the spinach for 2 minutes or until wilted. Refresh under cold running water until cool, then squeeze to remove excess water. Finely chop and place in a bowl with the yogurt, 1 garlic clove and the juice of ½ lemon. Season with salt and pepper and stir until combined. Set aside.

In a saucepan, bring the hot stock and bulgur wheat to the boil, then stir in the turmeric and reduce the heat to low. Simmer, covered with a lid, for 10 minutes or until the bulgur is just tender but retains a little bite. Drain and set aside until ready to use.

Heat the remaining oil in a large, deep sauté pan over a medium heat and fry the onions for 8 minutes, stirring regularly, until tender. Reduce the heat to low, add the remaining garlic and cook for 1 minute. Stir in the spice mix, the remaining spinach and the lemon zest and cook for a couple of minutes until the spinach has wilted, then remove from the heat.

Add the bulgur to the sauté pan with the remaining lemon juice and roasted squash. Season with salt and pepper, to taste, and turn gently until combined. Pile the pilaf into a serving bowl, scatter over the mint and serve with the spinach yogurt sauce.

· · · · · · · · · · · · · · · · · · · ·
PART-TIME VARIATION

Autumn squash pilaf with chicken in yogurt sauce This chicken in spiced yogurt is a bit like a Middle Eastern version of coronation chicken. Mix together 80g/2¾oz/⅓ cup Greek-style yogurt with 3 tbsp mayonnaise. Stir in 2 tsp baharat spice mix and the juice of 1 lemon. Stir in 400g/14oz shredded cooked chicken, season and turn until combined. Serve on top of the pilaf instead of the spinach yogurt sauce.

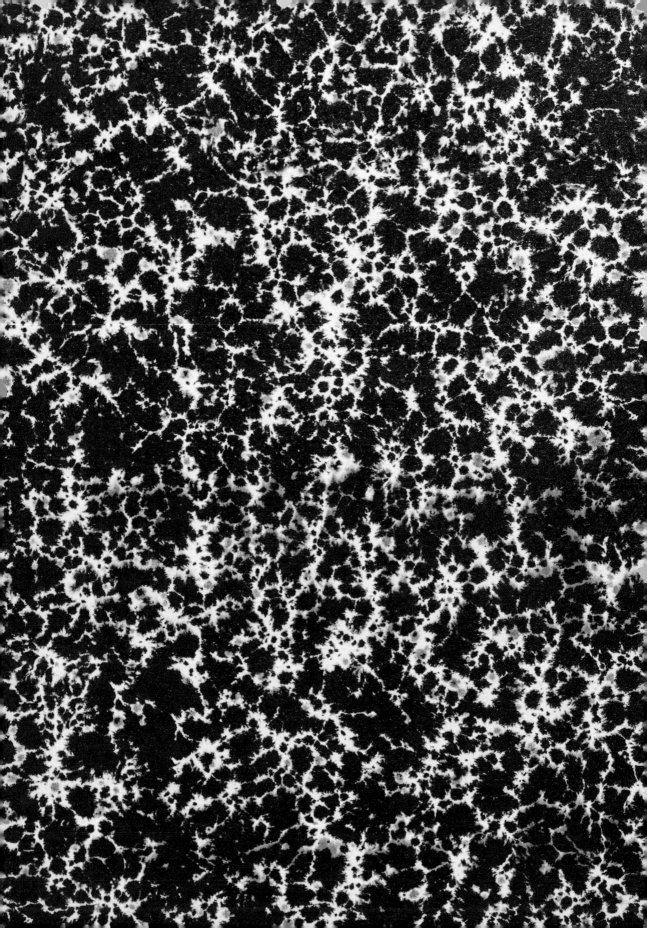

Winter

A time to hunker down and soothe the soul with heart-warming soups, stews, bakes and roasts. Even at this time of the year you can rely on fresh vegetables (and fruit) to add a splash of colour to your cooking, from deep crimson radicchio/endive and purple-hued red cabbage to vibrant green Brussels sprouts and radiant orange citrus fruit. Brassicas and root vegetables love the chill of winter and they are at their seasonal best now.

Seasonal vegetables:

Beetroot/beets (in season)

Brussels sprout (peak)

Cabbage, green/red/white/Savoy (peak)

Carrot (peak)

Cauliflower (in season)

Cavolo nero (peak)

Celeriac/celery root (peak)

Celery (peak)

Chard (in season)

Chicory/Belgian endive (peak)

Greens (peak)

Jerusalem artichoke (peak)

Kale (peak)

Leek (peak)

Lettuce (peak)

Mushroom (in season)

Onion (peak)

Onion, spring/scallion (in season)

Parsnip (peak)

Potato (peak)

Pumpkin and squash (peak)

Purple sprouting broccoli (in season)

Radicchio/endive (peak)

Rocket/arugula (in season)

Shallot (peak)

Spinach (in season)

Swede/rutabaga (peak)

Sweet potato (peak)

Turnip (peak)

Watercress (in season)

Radicchio with Thai flavours

What I crave most in the winter months is colour, crunch and lively flavours, and these stuffed radicchio leaves are all that. Dusky-red radicchio leaves are the perfect 'container' for a filling of sweet pineapple, hot chillies, fragrant kaffir lime leaves and crunchy peanuts. This makes an elegant first course, canapé, snack or light lunch.

Serves **4**
Preparation time: **15 minutes**

300g/3½oz/2 cups prepared fresh pineapple, diced

3 kaffir lime leaves, thinly shredded

1–2 red bird's eye chillies, deseeded and diced

1 large handful of fresh mint leaves, finely chopped

juice of 1 large lime, plus extra wedges, to serve

12 large radicchio or Little Gem/ Bibb lettuce leaves, stalk-ends trimmed

2 tbsp toasted coconut shavings

55g/2oz/½ cup salted roasted peanuts, finely chopped

Mix together the pineapple, kaffir lime, 1 of the chillies, mint and lime juice. Spoon the mixture into the hollow of each radicchio or lettuce leaf. Arrange the leaves on a platter and scatter over the coconut shavings, peanuts and the remaining chilli, if you like extra heat. Serve with lime wedges on the side.

. . . .
PART-TIME VARIATIONS

Radicchio with Thai prawns For an alternative filling, fry 200g/7oz chopped peeled raw tiger prawns/jumbo shrimp in 1 tbsp coconut oil with 3 shredded kaffir lime leaves, 1 diced deseeded red bird's eye chilli and 1 finely chopped lemongrass stalk for 2 minutes, or until the prawns/shrimp are pink. Remove from the heat and add the juice of 1 lime and season with salt and pepper. Spoon the mixture into the radicchio leaves and scatter over 1 diced deseeded red bird's eye chilli, if you like, and 2 tbsp chopped fresh mint leaves. Finish with unsalted, chopped roasted cashews scattered over the top.

Radicchio with Thai pork For a pork filling, fry 150g/5½oz minced/ ground pork in 1 tbsp coconut oil for 10 minutes until crisp and golden. Add 2 finely chopped garlic cloves, 3 shredded kaffir lime leaves, 1 diced deseeded red bird's eye chilli and 1 finely chopped lemongrass stalk and cook for another 2 minutes. Remove from the heat and add the juice of 1 lime and season with salt and pepper. Spoon the mixture into the radicchio leaves and scatter over 1 diced deseeded red bird's eye chilli, if you like, and 2 tbsp chopped fresh mint leaves. Finish with unsalted, chopped roasted cashews scattered over the top.

Black rice, pineapple, mint and tofu salad

Pineapple is one of the few fruits that is in season over the winter months – perfect timing, just when many of us are feeling slightly jaded and are in need of a vitamin C boost. The perfect balance of hot, salty, sweet, sour, crunchy and soft, this main-meal, Asian-style salad is sure to get the tastebuds going. Black rice not only adds a dramatic contrast of colour, it has a lovely nutty texture, too. Who said salads are just for summer?

Serves **4**
Preparation time: **15 minutes**
Cooking time: **30 minutes**

280g/9oz/1½ cups black rice, rinsed well

75g/2½oz curly kale, tough stalks removed, torn into small bite-size pieces

2 spring onions/scallions, thinly sliced diagonally

1 small red pepper, deseeded and diced

200g/7oz prepared fresh pineapple, cut into bite-size pieces

175g/6oz silken tofu, drained and cut into bite-size cubes

2 handfuls of mint leaves, chopped

2 handfuls of basil leaves

1 medium-hot red chilli, deseeded and diced

55g/2oz/½ cup salted roasted cashew nuts, roughly chopped

sea salt and freshly ground black pepper

Dressing

125ml/4½fl oz/½ cup coconut milk

finely grated zest of 1 unwaxed lime and the juice of 2 limes

2.5cm/1in piece of fresh root ginger, peeled and finely grated

¾ tsp caster/superfine sugar

Put the rice in a pan and pour in enough cold water to cover by 1.5cm/⅝in, then season with salt. Bring to the boil, turn the heat to its lowest setting, cover with a lid and simmer for 30 minutes until the rice is tender. Drain if needed and leave to rest for 5 minutes, covered, then leave to cool slightly.

Meanwhile, mix together all the ingredients for the dressing and season. Set aside.

Tip the rice onto a large serving plate. Add the kale, spring onions/scallions, red pepper and pineapple and turn gently until combined. Top with the tofu, herbs, chilli and cashews, and spoon the dressing over just before serving.

PART-TIME VARIATIONS

Black rice, pineapple, mint and salmon salad Swap the tofu for 2 fillets cooked wild salmon, skin removed and broken into flakes.

Alternatively, this salad is a perfect way to use up leftover roast meats, such as chicken, pork or beef, cut into thin slices.

Celeriac, sesame and ginger bhajis
with coriander dipping sauce

Celeriac/celery root is such a wacky-looking vegetable, but don't be fooled by this knobbly, odd-shaped root – it is incredibly versatile with a pleasing nutty, celery-like flavour. Roast it, boil it, mash it or eat it raw. It makes a great base for these golden fried vegetable bhajis.

Makes **18**
Preparation time: **20 minutes**
Cooking time: **30 minutes**

250g/9oz (peeled weight) celeriac/celery root, coarsely grated
juice of ½ lemon
1 onion, coarsely grated
5cm/2in piece of fresh root ginger, coarsely grated
125g/4½oz/1 cup chickpea/gram flour
1 tsp sea salt
1 tbsp toasted sesame seeds
½ tsp ground turmeric
1 tbsp garam masala
1 tsp nigella seeds
sunflower oil, for frying

Coriander dipping sauce
2 handfuls of fresh coriander/ cilantro leaves, finely chopped
200g/7oz/scant 1 cup plain Greek-style yogurt
juice of 1 large lime
1 garlic clove, finely chopped
1 green chilli, diced
freshly ground black pepper

Put the celeriac/celery root in a mixing bowl, add the lemon juice and turn it with your hands until coated. The lemon juice will stop it discolouring. Stir in the onion and ginger.

In a separate bowl, mix together the chickpea/gram flour, salt, sesame seeds, turmeric, garam masala and nigella seeds. Gradually add the spiced flour to the celeriac/celery root, turning them with a fork until they are coated.

Mix together all the ingredients for the dipping sauce. Set aside.

Pour a 2cm/¾in depth of sunflower oil into a medium heavy-based saucepan and heat to 176°C/350°F (or until a cube of bread browns in 40 seconds).

Using a tablespoon, scoop up enough of the mixture to make a round about the size of a golf ball (you may wish to wear rubber gloves to avoid turmeric-stained hands). Fry the bhajis in batches for 3 minutes per batch, turning them halfway, until golden and cooked through. Drain on paper towels and keep warm in a low oven while you cook the rest of the bhajis – the mixture makes around 18 in total. Serve the bhajis warm with the dipping sauce on the side.

Pumpkin, chickpea and barley soup

〜〜〜〜〜〜〜〜〜〜〜〜〜〜〜〜〜〜〜〜〜〜〜

You can't beat this hearty soup for wholesomeness, and as it's made largely from storecupboard ingredients it's so easy to put together. If you have a wedge of Parmesan, remember to save the rind to add to soups such as this; it adds a rich umami flavour to the broth. Likewise, keep the seeds and strands from the middle of the pumpkin and bake for 30 minutes until dried and crisp, then blitz with sea salt to use as a condiment.

Serves **4**
Preparation time: **15 minutes**
Cooking time: **25 minutes**

75g/2½oz/scant ½ cup pearl barley, rinsed
2 tbsp olive oil, plus extra for drizzling
2 onions, roughly chopped
2 celery stalks, thinly sliced
4 garlic cloves, thinly sliced
600g/1lb 5oz prepared (skin and seeds removed) pumpkin or butternut squash
½ tsp dried chilli/hot pepper flakes
1 heaped tbsp finely chopped fresh rosemary
1 litre/35fl oz/4¼ cups good-quality hot vegetable stock
400g/14oz can chopped tomatoes
rind from vegetarian Parmesan cheese, plus some finely grated, to serve (optional)
125g/4½oz/scant 1 cup canned chickpeas/garbanzo beans, drained
Parsley Relish (see page 96), to serve (optional)
sea salt and freshly ground black pepper

Put the pearl barley in a saucepan and pour over enough water to cover generously. Bring to the boil, then reduce the heat and simmer for 20 minutes or until tender. Drain and set aside.

Meanwhile, heat the olive oil in a large saucepan over a medium-low heat, add the onions and cook for 7 minutes, until softened. Add the celery, garlic and pumpkin and cook for another 2 minutes. Stir in the dried chilli/hot pepper flakes and rosemary, then add the stock, chopped tomatoes and Parmesan rind, if you have one. Bring almost to the boil, then reduce the heat and simmer, part-covered with a lid, for 20 minutes or until the pumpkin is tender. Remove the Parmesan rind.

Using a potato masher, roughly mash the soup to break down the pumpkin and thicken the broth. Add the chickpeas/garbanzo beans and cooked barley, with a splash more stock, if needed, and heat through. Season with salt and pepper, to taste, and serve in bowls with a spoonful of parsley relish on top, an extra drizzle of oil and a grating of Parmesan.

· ·
PART-TIME VARIATIONS

Pumpkin, chicken and barley soup Swap the chickpeas/garbanzo beans for 2 chicken breasts, cut into bite-size chunks. Add to the pan 10 minutes before the end of the cooking time. If cooking for both vegetarians and flexitarians at the same time, halve the soup and add 60g/2¼oz/½ cup chickpeas/garbanzo beans to one half and 1 chicken breast to the other.

You could also add leftover roasted meat, such as chicken, lamb or beef, to the soup at the end of the cooking time just to heat it through instead of the chicken breast.

Japanese-style scrambled eggs with rice

~~~~~~

Dulse seaweed is a fairly recent discovery for me. While it's not essential here, it does add a savoury umami quality (some say it's a bit like bacon) to these softly scrambled eggs. It's also brimming with nutrients and is even rumoured to cure hangovers! Find dried dulse flakes in large supermarkets and Asian grocers. It's essential to cook the eggs gently and slowly so they remain moist. Serve, Japanese-style, on top of white rice with spinach and sesame seeds, or just enjoy as they are.

Preparation time: **10 minutes**
Cooking time: **8 minutes**

8 large eggs
1 tsp mirin or ½ tsp caster/
   superfine sugar
1½ tsp light soy sauce or tamari
1 tbsp toasted sesame oil
25g/1oz/1½ tbsp butter or dairy-
   free alternative
100g/3½oz spinach leaves
2 tsp toasted sesame seeds
2 tsp dried dulse flakes or nori
   flakes (optional)
¼ tsp shichimi togarashi
   (optional)
freshly ground black pepper
Jasmine or sushi rice, to serve
   (optional)

Break the eggs into a mixing bowl and beat with the mirin or caster/superfine sugar, soy sauce or tamari. Season with freshly ground black pepper.

Heat the sesame oil and butter or spread in a non-stick saucepan over a medium-low heat. Add the beaten egg mixture and cook over a low heat, stirring gently, until softly scrambled with large flakes of egg. It's best to slightly undercook the eggs, as they will continue to cook in the heat of the pan.

Meanwhile, steam the spinach until wilted, then squeeze out any excess water.

To serve, place the spinach on top of the rice, if using, and spoon the scrambled eggs on top. Finish with a sprinkling of sesame seeds, dulse or nori, and shichimi togarashi, if liked.

. . . .

PART-TIME VARIATION

Japanese-style scrambled tofu with rice Swap the eggs for 400g/14oz firm tofu, drained well, and roughly mashed with the back of a fork. Heat 1 tbsp sesame oil, 1 tbsp sunflower oil, 1 tbsp light soy sauce, 2 tsp mirin (or 1 tsp caster sugar) and ½ tsp ground turmeric in a saucepan over a medium heat, stirring. Add the tofu and cook, stirring, until combined with the sesame oil mixture and heated through, about 5–7 minutes. The tofu will become softer in texture as it cooks. Season with pepper and serve as above.

Parsnip, apple and potato soup
with winter pesto

This soup is surprisingly creamy and velvety, especially as there is no sign of dairy. To lend a contrast in texture, the potato and parsnip crisps make a great crunchy topping and are a perfect way to use up the veg peelings. Feel free to finish the soup with a scattering of vegetarian Caerphilly or other crumbly cheese, or a dairy-free equivalent, before serving, if you like.

Serves **4**
Preparation time: **10 minutes**
Cooking time: **25 minutes**

500g/1lb 2oz parsnips, scrubbed, peel pared into long, thin ribbons, then cut into chunks
300g/10½oz white potatoes, scrubbed, peel pared into long, thin ribbons, then cut into chunks
5 tbsp olive oil, plus extra for drizzling
2 onions, roughly chopped
5 garlic cloves, finely chopped
1 large apple, peeled, cored and chopped
3 tbsp finely chopped fresh rosemary
1.2 litres/40fl oz/5 cups good-quality vegetable stock
3 bay leaves
sea salt and freshly ground black pepper
warm crusty bread, to serve

Preheat the oven to 180°C/350°F/Gas 4.

To make the crisps, place the vegetable-peel ribbons on a large baking sheet, drizzle over a little oil and toss until well coated. Season with salt and pepper, then spread out evenly (use 2 baking sheets, if they look overcrowded) and roast for 25 minutes, turning them once or twice, until golden and crisp. Drain on paper towels and leave to cool and crisp up further.

To make the soup, heat 1 tablespoon of the oil in a large saucepan over a medium heat, add the onions and cook, part-covered and stirring occasionally, for 5 minutes. Reduce the heat slightly and stir in the parsnips, potatoes and 3 garlic cloves and cook for another 5 minutes. Add the apple, 1 tablespoon rosemary, stock and bay leaves, and bring to the boil, then reduce the heat slightly and simmer, covered, for 15 minutes or until the potatoes are tender.

To make the winter pesto, put the remaining 4 tablespoons oil in a mini food processor or blender. Add the remaining rosemary and garlic cloves, then pulse to a coarse oily paste. Season with salt and pepper.

Using a stick/immersion blender, blend the soup until smooth and creamy – add a splash more stock or water if needed. Serve topped with a spoonful of winter pesto and a handful of parsnip and potato crisps.

e-baked eggs with herb salsa

~~~~~~~~~~~~~~~~~~~~~~~~~~~~~~~~

all their various glorious forms tick the right
boxes when it comes to simple, warming and nutritious meals. A
complete meal in a pan, what more could you ask? Well, maybe
some crusty bread to mop up the sauce! The herb salsa isn't
essential, but it does take the flavour up a notch or two.

Serves **4**
Preparation time: **15 minutes**
Cooking time: **45 minutes**

2 tbsp extra virgin olive oil
1 white onion, finely chopped
1 red pepper, deseeded and finely
    chopped
4 garlic cloves, finely chopped
1 tsp chipotle chilli flakes or
    powder
1 tsp cumin seeds
2 x 400g/14oz cans chopped
    tomatoes
1 tsp sweet smoked paprika
2 tsp ground coriander
150g/5oz/1 cup canned black
    beans, drained and rinsed
juice of ½ lemon
4 large eggs
sea salt and freshly ground black
    pepper
1 large avocado, halved, skin and
    stone removed and sliced
    lengthways, to garnish

Herb salsa
2 large handfuls of fresh
    coriander/cilantro leaves, plus
    extra to serve
1 large handful of fresh flat-leaf
    parsley leaves
1 green jalapeño chilli, roughly
    chopped
1 garlic clove, minced
1 tsp cumin seeds
juice of ½ lemon

Heat the oil in an ovenproof, lidded sauté pan over a medium
heat, add the onion and red pepper and cook for 8 minutes until
softened, then add the garlic, chipotle and cumin and cook for
another 2 minutes.

Pour in the chopped tomatoes and 100ml/3½fl oz/scant ½ cup
water and bring up to a gentle boil. Add the ground spices and
reduce the heat to medium-low. Simmer for 25 minutes, part-
covered with a lid and stirring occasionally, until reduced and
thickened. The sauce should be thick enough to make a channel
when a spoon is drawn through it. Stir in the black beans and lemon
juice and season with salt and pepper, to taste.

Meanwhile, blend together all the ingredients for the herb salsa and
spoon it into a small serving bowl.

Preheat the grill/broiler to medium-high. Make 4 evenly spaced
indentations in the sauce and crack an egg into each one, keeping
the yolks intact. Place under the grill/broiler – not too close to the
heat – and grill for 10 minutes or until the egg whites are just set
and the yolks remain runny. Serve topped with avocado and the
herb salsa.

· ·

PART-TIME VARIATIONS

Chipotle-baked eggs with chorizo Chop 100g/3½oz chorizo
cooking sausage into small bite-size pieces and add to the pan with
the onion and pepper, then follow the recipe above.

Chipotle-baked eggs with humous For a vegan version, leave out
the eggs and use a full 400g/14oz can black beans. Just before
serving, top with avocado, a large spoonful of humous and a
smattering of smoked or toasted almonds.

Weekday dahl

My go-to meal when I'm looking for something sustaining, nutritious and tasty to eat, which is also hassle-free to make. Dahl is one of my absolute favourite dishes, and the simpler the better. Ginger, garlic, turmeric and chilli, with their immune-system-boosting properties, are all essentials at this time of year.

Serves **4**
Preparation time: **15 minutes**
Cooking time: **20 minutes**

250g/9oz/1⅓ cups split red lentils, rinsed well
3 bay leaves
150g/5½oz chard, stalks trimmed and sliced
1 tsp ground turmeric
juice of ½ lemon, plus a good squeeze, to serve
sea salt and freshly ground black pepper
plain Greek-style yogurt and warm wholemeal chapattis, to serve

Tarka
50g/1¾oz/3½ tbsp ghee, butter or coconut oil
3 garlic cloves, finely chopped
1 tsp cumin seeds
2 tsp garam masala
1 tsp dried chilli/hot pepper flakes

Put the lentils and bay leaves into a large saucepan with enough water to cover by 5cm/2in and bring to the boil, skimming off any froth that rises to the surface. Reduce the heat and simmer, part-covered, for 15 minutes, or until the lentils are tender and starting to break down. Add more hot water, if needed – you want the dahl to be quite sloppy, rather than thick and dry.

Meanwhile, make the tarka. Melt the ghee, butter or coconut oil in a small frying pan, add the garlic and fry for 2 minutes, until starting to colour, then stir in the cumin seeds, garam masala and chilli/hot pepper flakes and cook for another 1 minute.

Meanwhile, steam the chard leaves and stalks until just wilted and tender.

To finish the dahl, remove the bay leaves, stir in the turmeric and lemon juice, and season generously with salt and pepper – you definitely need more salt than you may think. Stir the tarka into the dahl. Spoon the dahl into serving bowls and top with a spoonful of yogurt, the chard and an extra squeeze of lemon juice.

PART-TIME VARIATIONS

Topping ideas Add leftover shredded roast chicken to the tarka mixture and warm through. Serve on top of the dahl, instead of stirred in, with a handful of coriander/cilantro leaves.

Add 150g/5½oz raw peeled tiger prawns/jumbo shrimp to the tarka mixture with the garlic and cook for 2 minutes, turning once, until pink. Serve on top of the dahl, instead of stirred in, with a handful of coriander/cilantro leaves.

Finish the dahl off with a poached egg or crisp fried cubes of paneer or tofu. Place on top of the chard before serving.

Red chicory salad with honey pecans

~~~~~~

Winter salads offer respite from the heavier dishes of the colder months and have an ability to revive a fatigued palate and enliven the appetite. This is a substantial salad with a combination of red Camargue rice and black wild rice at its base – I bought a bag of the grains already combined. The slight bitterness of the crisp red chicory is the perfect foil to the sweet crunch of the honey pecans. I've made more of the pecans than needed for the salad, as they also make a moreish snack.

Serves **4**
Preparation time: **15 minutes**
Cooking time: **25 minutes**

250g/9oz/1⅔ cups mixture of red Camargue rice and wild rice, rinsed
1 large apple, cored, diced and tossed in 1 tbsp lemon juice to stop browning
125g/4½oz red cabbage, shredded
3 red chicory leaves, sliced
sea salt

Dressing
juice of 1 lemon
4 tbsp extra virgin olive oil
4 tsp wholegrain mustard
sea salt and freshly ground black pepper

Honey pecans
4 tsp runny honey
1 tsp extra virgin olive oil
¼ tsp chilli powder
100g/3½oz/1 cup pecan halves
sea salt and freshly ground black pepper

Put the rice in a saucepan with enough water to cover by 1.5cm/⅝in, season with salt and bring to the boil. Reduce the heat to its lowest setting, cover with a lid and simmer for 25 minutes or until the rice is tender and the water has been absorbed. If the rice is still a little firm, add a splash of hot water, cover and cook for slightly longer. Leave to stand off the heat for 5 minutes, then fluff up the grains with a fork. Spoon the rice into a large serving bowl and set aside to cool to room temperature.

Meanwhile, preheat the oven to 150°C/300°F/Gas 2 and line a baking sheet with baking paper.

To make the honey pecans, warm the honey in a small pan, then remove from the heat. Stir in the olive oil and chilli powder, season with salt and pepper, then taste and add more chilli, if needed. Stir in the pecans until well coated. Tip the pecans onto the lined baking sheet, spread out evenly and roast for 15 minutes, until toasted and sticky. Leave to cool.

Mix together all the ingredients for the dressing and season. Spoon as much as needed over the rice, then turn until coated. Add the diced apple, red cabbage and chicory to the bowl and turn gently until combined with the rice. Scatter over half of the honey pecans, or as many as you like, and serve immediately. If you don't intend to serve the salad immediately, it's best to hold off adding the pecans until that point, as you don't want them to soften.

Warm lentil salad with roasted pears, blue cheese and pecans

〰〰〰〰〰〰〰〰〰〰〰〰〰〰〰〰〰〰〰〰〰

The sweet softness of the roasted pears is perfect with the crunch of the toasted pecans and bite of the cavolo nero (or you could use kale) and lentils. Choose pears that are just on the right side of ripeness; too soft and they'll fall apart when roasted. It is a salad that is best served slightly warm or at room temperature, but definitely not refrigerator cold.

Serves **4**
Preparation time: **15 minutes**
Cooking time: **45 minutes**

3 tbsp extra virgin olive oil
100g/3½oz cavolo nero or kale, tough stalks removed, leaves torn into large bite-size pieces
40g/1½oz/⅓ cup pecan halves
4 smallish red onions, peeled, root-ends trimmed, each cut into 6 wedges
4 just-ripe pears, peeled, cored, each cut into 6 wedges
juice of 1 lemon
270g/9½oz/scant 1½ cups dried puy lentils, rinsed
75g/2½oz vegetarian blue cheese, such as Dolcelatte, crumbled (optional)
2 handfuls of fresh dill or fennel fronds, torn into small sprigs, to garnish

Dressing
2 tbsp apple cider vinegar
1 tsp runny honey
1 tsp Dijon mustard
1 garlic clove, crushed
sea salt and freshly ground black pepper

Preheat the oven to 150°C/300°F/Gas 2. Rub 1 teaspoon of the oil into the cavolo nero leaves until lightly coated all over. Spread out on a baking sheet and roast for 15 minutes, turning once, until crisp. At the same time, scatter the pecans onto a baking sheet and toast in the oven for 10–12 minutes, turning once, until they start to smell toasted. Roughly chop the pecans and set aside with the cavolo nero.

Turn the oven up to 200°C/400°F/Gas 6. Put the onions on a baking sheet, toss in a little oil and roast for 25–30 minutes until tender. At the same time, toss the pears in the lemon juice and place on a baking sheet lined with baking paper. Roast for 20–25 minutes until soft and slightly golden.

Meanwhile, cook the puy lentils in a pan of boiling water for 25 minutes or until tender. Drain and tip into a serving bowl. Mix all the ingredients for the dressing with any remaining oil and season. Spoon half of the dressing over the lentils, and turn until combined.

To finish the salad, top the lentils with the red onions, cavolo nero and roasted pears. Scatter over the pecans and blue cheese, if using. Season and serve with the remaining dressing spooned over and the dill or fennel fronds to finish.

• •

PART-TIME VARIATIONS

Warm lentil salad with roasted pears, cashew cheese and pecans For a vegan alternative, use maple syrup instead of honey in the dressing and a cashew cheese in place of the blue cheese. You could also top with blobs of the Cashew Cream Cheese on page 94.

Warm lentil salad with roasted pears, pork and pecans Leftover roast pork makes a good alternative to the blue cheese. If you don't have any leftovers, try pork loin fillets. Season and pan-fry for a couple of minutes in a little olive oil until browned all over, then finish off in the oven for 10–15 minutes at the same time as you roast the pears, until cooked but still a little pink in the middle.

Slow-cooked pulled celeriac
with roast garlic cream

Don't be put off by the long list of ingredients here; the celeriac/celery root is easy to prepare and can pretty much be left alone to roast in the oven until ready. You'll have more barbecue sauce than you need for this recipe and any left over will keep happily in the refrigerator in a lidded container for up to 1 month.

Serves **4**
Preparation time: **30 minutes**
Cooking time: **1½ hours**

750g/1lb 10oz celeriac/celery root, peeled and cut into wedges
1 tbsp olive oil
juice of 1 small lemon
sea salt and freshly ground black pepper

Barbecue sauce
2 tsp chipotle chilli flakes
2 tbsp apple cider vinegar
2 tbsp soft dark brown sugar
100ml/3½fl oz/scant ½ cup tomato ketchup
1 tbsp dark soy sauce
1 tbsp English mustard
juice of 2 oranges
1 tsp allspice
2 tsp ground cumin
2 tsp smoked paprika
1 tsp dried oregano

Roast garlic cream
4 whole garlic cloves, unpeeled
150ml/5fl oz/scant ¾ cup thick sour cream
2 tbsp mayonnaise
juice of 1 lime

To serve
4–8 soft corn tortillas
thinly sliced Little Gem/Bibb lettuce, red cabbage and red onion
fresh coriander/cilantro leaves
lime wedges

Preheat the oven to 180°C/350°F/Gas 4.

In a large baking dish, toss the celeriac/celery root in the olive oil and lemon juice until coated. Season with salt and pepper, cover with foil and roast for 1 hour, turning halfway, until tender. At the same time as turning the celeriac/celery root, wrap the whole garlic cloves in a foil parcel, place on a baking sheet and roast for 30 minutes until tender.

Meanwhile, put all the ingredients for the barbecue sauce in a saucepan. Stir in 200ml/7fl oz/scant 1 cup water and bring almost to the boil. Reduce the heat to low and simmer for 5 minutes or until reduced and thickened.

When the celeriac/celery root is tender, transfer it to a baking sheet and remove the garlic from the oven. Shred the celeriac/celery root into strips using 2 forks. Spoon over some of the sauce to lightly coat the celeriac/celery root, turning it until combined and return to the oven for 20–25 minutes until golden and crisp in places.

To make the garlic cream, squeeze the roasted garlic cloves out of their skins into a bowl. Mash with a fork, then stir in the sour cream, mayonnaise and lime juice. Season with salt and pepper and set aside.

To serve, warm the tortillas in the oven and reheat any remaining barbecue sauce in a small pan. Arrange some shredded lettuce and red cabbage in the middle of each tortilla, spoon on some of the celeriac/celery root and drizzle over a little extra sauce. Top with a spoonful of the roast garlic cream, a few slices of red onion and some coriander/cilantro leaves. Serve with wedges of lime for squeezing over.

PART-TIME VARIATION

Slow-roast pulled pork This is probably the only full-on meat dish in this book. Since the pork in this recipe requires a long time to roast, it seems logical to me to make the most of the heat of the oven. Any leftover roasted pork will keep for up to 3 days in the refrigerator.

Preheat the oven to 160°C/315°F/Gas 2–3. Cut 700g/1lb 9oz pork shoulder joint into 4 pieces. Heat 2 tbsp olive oil in a large casserole dish, add the pork and brown for 5 minutes, turning it until browned all over. Remove the pork from the casserole and add 200ml/7fl oz/ scant 1 cup water, stirring to dislodge any caramelized bits stuck to the base of the pan. Add the barbecue sauce and heat to boiling point, stirring. Return the pork to the casserole, spoon the sauce over, cover with a lid and place in the oven for 2½ hours or until the meat starts to fall apart.

Remove the pork from the casserole, cover with foil and leave to rest for 10 minutes. Heat the sauce on the hob until reduced and thickened. Shred the pork using 2 forks, then spoon over enough of the sauce to coat. Serve as left, with all the various accompaniments and warmed tortillas.

Chickpea tofu
with broccoli and ginger miso dressing

Burmese in origin, chickpea tofu is a great alternative to the soy-based version. Slightly denser in texture, it retains that familiar smooth, creamy texture of tofu. I've kept this version unadulterated, with just ground turmeric for colour, but you could add spices, herbs or garlic powder to the tofu for extra flavour.

Serves **4**
Preparation time: **20 minutes,**
plus 1 hour chilling
Cooking time: **36 minutes**

165g/5¾oz/1⅓ cups chickpea/ gram flour
½ tsp ground turmeric
1 tsp sea salt
sunflower oil, for greasing
350g/12oz head of broccoli, cut into florets; stalks cut into batons
1 handful of fresh coriander/ cilantro leaves, chopped
50g/1¾oz/⅓ cup roasted unsalted peanuts
2 spring onions/scallions, thinly sliced diagonally
1 medium-hot red chilli, thinly sliced diagonally
cooked jasmine rice and lime wedges, to serve

Ginger miso dressing
3 tbsp sesame oil
2 tbsp rice vinegar
1 tbsp light soy sauce
2 tsp soft light brown sugar
1 tbsp white miso
5cm/2in piece of fresh root ginger, peeled and finely grated
1 large garlic clove, finely grated
½ tsp dried chilli/hot pepper flakes
freshly ground black pepper

Start by making the chickpea tofu. Line a 23cm/9in square baking pan with cling film/plastic wrap. In a saucepan, gradually add the chickpea/gram flour, turmeric and salt to 250ml/9fl oz/1 cup water, stirring continuously with a balloon whisk until combined. Leave to sit for 10 minutes, stirring occasionally.

Place the pan over a medium heat and gradually add 500ml/17fl oz/2 cups hot water, stirring continuously with a balloon whisk. When the mixture reaches simmering point, reduce the heat slightly and switch over to a wooden spoon. Cook, stirring continuously, for 6 minutes, or until thickened to a similar consistency as thick polenta/cornmeal – it will look as though it is turning lumpy, but keep stirring until the mixture becomes smooth and creamy. Tip the mixture into the prepared pan and evenly smooth out until about 1cm/½in thick. Chill for about 1 hour (if making in advance, it will keep for up to 4 days in the refrigerator) until firm.

When ready to serve, preheat the oven to 200°C/400°F/Gas 6. Cut the tofu into large bite-size cubes and place on a greased baking sheet. Brush with oil and bake for 25–30 minutes until it starts to crisp and puff up slightly.

Meanwhile, mix together all the ingredients for the sauce with 2 tablespoons hot water in a small pan. Season with pepper and gently warm through.

Steam the broccoli for 5 minutes or until tender.

To serve, divide the broccoli between 4 shallow serving bowls and spoon over some of the dressing. Top with the tofu, coriander/ cilantro, peanuts, spring onions/scallions and chilli. Serve with the remaining dressing, jasmine rice and wedges of lime on the side.

· ·

PART-TIME VARIATION

White fish with broccoli and ginger miso dressing Swap the tofu with 4 thick fillets white fish, such as hake. Pan-fry in a mixture of butter and olive oil for 5–8 minutes, until opaque. Serve as above.

Winter green noodles with tempeh crumbs

≈≈≈≈≈≈≈≈≈≈≈≈≈≈≈≈≈≈≈≈≈≈≈≈≈≈≈≈≈≈≈

I have always struggled to like tempeh – I thought I should like it, after all I love tofu, but I think it was mainly a textural thing. This recipe has changed my mind. I've discovered the secret is to crumble it into small pieces, then stir-fry until golden and flavour it with a mixture of soy and spices. *Shichimi togarashi* – sometimes called by its first name or *nanami* – is a fragrant, chilli-hot Japanese spice mix that also features roasted orange peel, seaweed and ginger. It's one of my favourite ways to add a blast of flavour and heat.

Serves **4**
Preparation time: **10 minutes**
Cooking time: **10 minutes**

200g/7oz tempeh
2 tbsp sunflower oil
2 tbsp sesame oil
2 tbsp light soy sauce
2 tsp shichimi togarashi
100g/3½oz curly kale, tough
    stalks removed
100g/3½oz green cabbage or
    greens, shredded
75g/2½oz Brussels sprouts, thinly
    sliced
3 garlic cloves, thinly sliced
600g/1lb 5oz cooked medium
    udon noodles
1 tsp toasted sesame seeds
sea salt and freshly ground black
    pepper

Crumble the tempeh into very small pieces, about the size of a chickpea/garbanzo bean. Heat half of the sunflower oil and sesame oil in a large wok or frying pan over a medium-high heat. Add the tempeh, spreading it out as much as possible, and leave it to brown for a couple of minutes. Stir, then cook until light golden all over. Add half of the soy sauce and togarashi and stir-fry for another 2 minutes until crisp. Tip it into a bowl and keep warm in a low oven.

Wipe the wok or pan, then heat the remaining oils, add the kale, cabbage, sprouts and garlic and stir-fry for 3 minutes, or until the vegetables have wilted but are still slightly crisp. Add the noodles, separating them with your fingers, then the remaining soy sauce, togarashi and a splash of water. Cook briefly until warmed through, then season with salt and pepper. Serve the noodles, sprinkled with the tempeh and the sesame seeds.

· ·

PART-TIME VARIATION

Winter green noodles with duck Replace the tempeh with 2 small duck breasts, skin patted dry and scored in a criss-cross pattern. Season the duck breasts and place them skin-side down in a cold, dry frying pan, then heat the pan slowly. Fry the breasts, letting the fat run out and the skin crisp up for about 10 minutes, then turn the duck over and cook for another 5 minutes until the meat is browned all over but the inside is still pink. Leave the duck to rest while you cook the winter greens and noodles as above, using only half of the oils, soy sauce and togarashi. Slice the duck and serve on top of the winter greens stir-fry.

...ed one-pan sweet potato hash

~~~~~~

...ig fan of one-pan roasts. This one is a combination of sweet potatoes, red onions, parsnips, cauliflower, chickpeas/garbanzo beans and smoked tofu, with Indian spices and a roasted garlic raita. A fried egg placed on top of the hash before serving is always a good option, but it's also just as nice without.

Serves **4**
Preparation time: **15 minutes**
Cooking time: **45 minutes**

780g/1lb 10oz sweet potatoes, peeled and cut into large bite-size chunks

5 small red onions, trimmed, each cut into 6 wedges

2 parsnips, peeled, halved and cut into wedges

1 small cauliflower, broken into florets

6 bay leaves

225g/8oz smoked tofu, drained and cut into bite-size cubes

100g/3½oz/¾ cup canned chickpeas/garbanzo beans, drained

150g/5½oz/⅔ cup plain Greek-style yogurt

Spice mix

5 tbsp olive oil

1½ tbsp garam masala

1 tsp ground turmeric

½ tsp dried chilli/hot pepper flakes

juice of 2 lemons

1 garlic bulb, cloves separated

sea salt and freshly ground black pepper

Preheat the oven to 200°C/400°F/Gas 6.

Combine all the ingredients for the spice mix in a large mixing bowl, using half of the lemon juice and adding 1 of the garlic cloves, crushed. Season with salt and pepper. Add the sweet potatoes, red onions, parsnips and cauliflower and turn to coat everything in the spice mix. Transfer to 2 large roasting pans, spread out evenly, tuck in the bay leaves and roast for 20 minutes. Reserve any marinade left in the bowl as this will be used to flavour the yogurt.

Remove the pans from the oven, divide the tofu, chickpeas/garbanzo beans and remaining garlic cloves between the 2 pans and turn until everything is combined. Roast for a further 25 minutes.

Squeeze the roasted garlic cloves out of their papery skins into a serving bowl and mash to a smooth paste. Add the yogurt to the bowl containing the reserved spice mix along with the remaining lemon juice and stir to combine. Add the spiced yogurt to the mashed garlic, along with a splash of water, and stir well until combined. Season with salt and pepper, to taste.

Serve the hash scattered with the coriander/cilantro and with a spoonful of the roast garlic raita.

. . . .

PART-TIME VARIATION

Roasted one-pan sweet potato and chicken hash Swap the smoked tofu with 4 chicken thighs. Add the vegetables to the spice mix and place them in the roasting pans, then repeat with the chicken. Roast as above and serve with the roast garlic raita.

Winter white pizza

〜〜〜〜〜〜〜〜〜〜〜〜〜〜〜〜〜〜〜〜〜〜

This was a new experiment for me, but I'm really happy to say it went down well with everyone who tried it. The pizza is topped with a creamy purée of Jerusalem artichokes, Stilton cheese, walnuts, cavolo nero, sage and mushrooms, and when tasted together it's undeniable that these seasonal ingredients were made for each other. Funny-looking, knobbly Jerusalem artichokes are really worth a try if they're new to you. They're a bit of a hassle to peel (you may get away with just scrubbing them if the skins are particularly thin), but you'll be rewarded with their delicious nutty, creamy, earthy flavour. This makes four individual pizzas, but you can also make two large ones, if easier, and spread the dough out into large baking sheets.

Makes **4**
Preparation time: **30 minutes**, plus **2 hours** rising
Cooking time: **40 minutes**

Pizza bases

½ tsp caster/superfine sugar
1 tsp fast-action/instant active dried yeast
550g/1lb 4oz/scant 4 cups '00' flour or strong white bread flour, plus extra for dusting
1½ tsp sea salt
2 tbsp olive oil, plus extra for drizzling

Topping

450g/1lb Jerusalem artichokes, peeled or scrubbed and cut into large chunks
3 large garlic cloves, peeled and left whole
4 tbsp double/heavy cream
½ tsp vegetable bouillon powder
1 red onion, thinly sliced into rings
4 mushrooms, thinly sliced
1 handful of fresh sage leaves
60g/2oz cavolo nero, tough stalks removed, leaves torn into pieces
100g/3½oz vegetarian Stilton cheese, crumbled (optional)
40g/1½oz/⅓ cup walnut pieces
salt and freshly ground black pepper

First, make the pizza bases. Pour 150ml/5fl oz/⅔ cup lukewarm water into a small bowl and stir in the sugar until dissolved. Sprinkle over the yeast and stir well until mixed in. Leave to stand for 15 minutes, until frothy.

Meanwhile, sift the flour and salt into a large mixing bowl, make a well in the middle and pour in the oil. Stir the yeast mixture before adding it to the bowl with another 200ml/7fl oz/scant 1 cup lukewarm water. Mix with a fork and then use your hands to bring the mixture together into a ball of dough – add more water if the dough is too dry or conversely a little extra flour. Tip the dough out onto a lightly floured work surface and knead for 5 minutes until smooth and it springs back quickly when pressed. Coat in a little oil and place in a clean bowl. Cover with cling film/plastic wrap and leave until doubled in size, about 1½ hours.

While the dough is proving, start to make the topping. Cook the Jerusalem artichokes in boiling salted water until tender, about 15 minutes. Drain and tip into a blender with the cream, bouillon powder and 3 tablespoons water, then blend until smooth and creamy – add a splash more cream or water if the purée is too thick; it should be a similar consistency to humous. Taste and season with salt and pepper, to taste. Set aside while you prepare the rest of the topping ingredients.

When the dough has risen, knock it back, pressing it down with your knuckles until deflated, then briefly knead again. Form the dough into 4 balls, cover with a clean cloth and set aside for 30 minutes.

Recipe continued overleaf ...

Winter white pizza continued ...

Preheat the oven to 240°C/450°F/Gas 8. Heat a pizza stone(s) or large baking sheet(s) until very hot.

Roll out a ball of dough on a lightly floured work surface into a thin round. Spoon a quarter of the artichoke purée on top, leaving a border around the edge. Top with a quarter of the onion, mushrooms, sage, cavolo nero, Stilton, if using, and walnuts. Drizzle over a little extra olive oil, season with pepper, and bake for 12 minutes until the base is crisp and golden. Repeat to make 4 pizzas in total – you may need to cook them in 2 batches.

. . . .

PART-TIME VARIATIONS

Dairy-free winter white pizza Instead of the cream in the Jerusalem artichoke purée, soak 55g/2oz/scant ½ cup cashew nuts in warm water for 1 hour, until softened. Boil the Jerusalem artichokes following the method on page 186 and tip them into a blender with the drained cashews, 6 tbsp water, 2 tbsp nutritional yeast flakes and ¾ tsp vegetable bouillon powder. Blend until smooth and creamy, adding more water if the purée is too thick. Leave out the Stilton and top with small spoonfuls of Cashew Cream Cheese (see page 94) or perhaps a vegan pesto.

Other topping ideas Pizza is a perfect meal in the flexitarian kitchen if you are catering for a range of tastes. Feel free to swap the suggested toppings with your own favourites, such as slices of prosciutto; anchovies; leftover cooked meats; seafood; roasted vegetables; olives; or an egg cracked on top – there are far too many options to mention.

Rich lentil ragu

~~~~~~

Red wine, sun-dried tomatoes and dark miso add great depth and richness to this meat-free ragu sauce. Serve the sauce with pasta, such as tagliatelle, or polenta/cornmeal – it also makes a great base for a vegetarian/vegan lasagne or moussaka. The ragu freezes well, so it's well worth making a double quantity to freeze in portions.

Serves **4–6**
Preparation time: **15 minutes**
Cooking time: **55 minutes**

2 tbsp olive oil
2 onions, roughly chopped
1 large carrot, finely chopped
1 celery stalk, finely chopped
3 garlic cloves, finely chopped
125g/4½oz/generous ½ cup Puy lentils, rinsed
175ml/6fl oz/generous ⅔ cup red wine (optional)
400ml/14fl oz/1⅔ cups good-quality vegetable stock
400g/14oz can chopped tomatoes
1 tbsp dark miso paste
60g/2¼oz sun-dried tomatoes in oil, drained and roughly chopped
1 tbsp chopped fresh rosemary
1 tsp dried oregano
2 bay leaves
sea salt and freshly ground black pepper

Heat the olive oil in a large saucepan over a medium heat, add the onions and cook, stirring occasionally, for 8 minutes until softened. Add the carrot, celery and garlic and cook for another 5 minutes. Stir in the lentils, then add the wine, if using. Let the wine bubble away until there is no aroma of alcohol. (If you're not using wine, up the quantity of stock.)

Add the rest of the ingredients, apart from the salt and pepper, and bring almost to boiling point. Reduce the heat, part-cover with a lid, and simmer for 40 minutes, stirring occasionally, until the lentils are tender. Remove the lid if the sauce is too thin, but cover the pan completely if the sauce begins to dry up. Season with salt and pepper, to taste.

• •

PART-TIME VARIATION

Rich beef ragu Use 55g/2oz/¼ cup lentils and 125g/4½oz minced/ground beef. Add the meat to the pan with the carrot, celery and garlic before the lentils and cook, breaking it up with a fork, for 5 minutes or until browned. Add the lentils and continue with the recipe, as above.

Turkish-style spiced pinto beans

～～～～～～～～～～～～～～～～～～

This warming hotpot is served with wholemeal couscous, although bulgur wheat, spelt, quinoa, rice or flatbreads would be equally good. Pul biber, also known as Aleppo pepper or Turkish chilli flakes, is made from crushed dried red peppers and can vary in heat from blisteringly hot to mild and fragrant. It's available from Middle Eastern shops, large supermarkets and online, but feel free to use dried chilli/hot pepper flakes instead, if more convenient.

Serves **4**
Preparation time: **10 minutes**
Cooking time: **20 minutes**

3 tbsp extra virgin olive oil

1 large onion, finely chopped

1 carrot, cut into small dice

3 garlic cloves, finely chopped

2 tsp cumin seeds

2 tsp coriander seeds, crushed

1 tsp ground turmeric

1 tsp hot pul biber or dried chilli/
   hot pepper flakes

2 x 400g/14oz cans pinto beans,
   chickpeas/garbanzo beans or
   kidney beans, drained

2 heaped tbsp tomato purée/
   paste

3 vine tomatoes, roughly
   chopped

1 unwaxed lemon, halved

150g/5½oz baby spinach

sea salt and freshly ground black
   pepper

cooked wholewheat couscous
   and thick Greek-style yogurt
   or humous, to serve

Heat the oil in a pan over a medium heat, add the onion and carrot and cook for 8 minutes, stirring often, until softened. Add the garlic, cumin and coriander seeds and cook for another 1 minute. Stir in the turmeric, pul biber and beans, ensuring they are well coated in the spice mix, and cook for a further 1 minute.

Add the tomato purée/paste, tomatoes and 300ml/10½fl oz/1¼ cups water. Bring almost to the boil, then reduce the heat to low and cook for 8 minutes, part-covered and stirring occasionally. Squeeze in the juice of the lemon, adding the lemon halves to the pan.

Add a third of the spinach, then stir in the next batch when the leaves have wilted down, followed by the remaining leaves. Cook for 2 minutes or until the spinach is tender. Season with salt and pepper, to taste, and check it is chilli-hot enough for you. Serve with couscous, topped with a spoonful of yogurt or humous.

Crumb-coated mushroom burgers
with root slaw

Try to find the largest, flattest mushrooms for these burgers. Portobello are usually best as they tend to be flatter with less of a curved cap than some others. Rather than waste the stalks, save them to make a mushroom stock or chop and add to stir-fries or stews. Try serving the burgers in a toasted brioche bun with all your favourite extras and sauces with the slaw by the side. Or instead of the extras, add a few spoonfuls of the slaw to the bun instead.

Serves **4**
Preparation time: **20 minutes**
Cooking time: **30–35 minutes**

50g/1¾oz/generous ⅓ cup plain/
    all-purpose flour
1 tsp smoked paprika
2 eggs, lightly beaten
50g/1¾oz/generous 1 cup dried
    panko breadcrumbs
1 tsp dried thyme
4 large, flat portobello
    mushrooms, stalks removed
olive oil, for drizzling
sea salt and freshly ground black
    pepper
4 toasted brioche buns, to serve

Root slaw
250g/9oz/scant 1½ cups plain
    Greek-style yogurt
1 tsp Dijon mustard
juice of 1 small lemon
2 carrots, coarsely grated
1 turnip, coarsely grated
200g/7oz red cabbage, finely
    shredded
½ small red onion, thinly sliced

Preheat the oven to 200°C/400°F/Gas 6. Put the flour on a plate and stir in the paprika and season with salt and pepper. Lightly beat the eggs in a shallow bowl. Put the breadcrumbs on a separate plate and stir in the thyme.

Dust the mushrooms, one at a time, in the flour until lightly coated, dunk into the egg and then the breadcrumbs until coated all over and place on a greased baking sheet. Drizzle a little oil over each one and cook in the oven for 30–35 minutes, turning once, until the outside is crisp and golden.

Meanwhile, make the slaw. Mix together the yogurt, Dijon and lemon juice, then season with salt and pepper. Put the vegetables in a bowl, spoon the dressing over and turn until combined.

Serve the mushroom burgers in a toasted brioche bun with all your favourite extras and sauces and with the slaw on the side.

Baked cavolo nero, leek and porcini pasta

It's not for the first time that I've sung the praises of dried porcini mushrooms. They may seem pricey at first glance, but a little goes a long way in terms of flavour, and they are so versatile. Cavolo nero, or black cabbage, is a dark-leaved cousin of curly kale and is perfect for a bake as it holds its own without wilting to insignificance. The beauty of this dish is that it can be made up to a day or two in advance, then finished off in the oven just before serving.

Serves **4**
Preparation time: **20 minutes**
Cooking time: **1 hour**

20g/¾oz dried porcini
    mushrooms
350g/12oz dried conchiglie pasta
    shells
250g/9oz cavolo nero, tough
    stalks removed, leaves torn
    into large bite-size pieces
2 tbsp olive oil, plus extra if
    needed
500g/1lb 2oz chestnut/cremini
    mushrooms, sliced
2 leeks, chopped
2 garlic cloves, finely chopped
50g/1¾oz/3½ tbsp dairy-free
    spread or butter
4 tbsp plain/all-purpose flour
1 litre/35fl oz/4¼ cups nut milk
    or other dairy-free milk or
    cow's milk
1 tbsp English mustard
4 tbsp nutritional yeast flakes
    or vegetarian hard cheese,
    grated
1 tbsp chopped fresh rosemary
2 tsp fresh thyme leaves or 1 tsp
    dried
40g/1½oz/⅓ cup chopped
    walnuts
sea salt and freshly ground black
    pepper

Soak the porcini in 150ml/5fl oz/⅔ cup just-boiled water for 20 minutes until softened. Drain, reserving the soaking liquid. Squeeze the mushrooms to remove any excess liquid and tear into pieces.

Meanwhile, cook the pasta in plenty of salted boiling water following the package directions, until *al dente*. Add the cavolo nero 1 minute before the pasta is ready. Drain the pasta and greens and refresh under cold running water. Set aside.

Heat the oil in a large sauté pan over a medium heat, add the mushrooms and soaked porcini and fry for 10 minutes, or until starting to turn golden and there is no liquid in the pan. Reduce the heat slightly, add the leeks and garlic (add a splash more oil if needed) and sauté for another 5 minutes.

To make the white sauce, melt the spread or butter in a saucepan over a medium-low heat. Reduce the heat, gradually add the flour, stirring with a balloon whisk, and cook for 1–2 minutes until the paste is golden. Strain the reserved porcini soaking liquid into the milk, then slowly pour it into the pan with the flour paste, whisking continuously. Add the mustard and season with salt and pepper. Cook, stirring, for 5 minutes or until thickened to the consistency of single/light cream. Stir in 3 tablespoons of the nutritional yeast flakes or cheese along with the herbs.

Meanwhile, preheat the oven to 220°C/425°F/Gas 7.

Tip the cooked pasta and cavolo nero into a large baking dish, add the mushroom and leek mixture, then pour over the sauce and turn until everything is thoroughly combined. Cover with foil and bake for 20 minutes, then remove the foil, scatter over the remaining nutritional yeast flakes or cheese along with the walnuts and return to the oven for 10 minutes or until golden on top.

Sweet potato gnocchi with butter sauce and hazelnuts

~~~~~~

Serves **4–6**
Preparation time: **30 minutes**
Cooking time: **1 hour 15 minutes**

Gnocchi can be fun to make with family or friends. It is best to bake the potatoes, rather than boil them, since you want to avoid adding any water as this will make the dough wet and fragile. Don't waste the potato skins; they can be transformed into crisps to serve with the gnocchi or dunked into dips.

450g/1lb sweet potatoes, wiped clean
750g/1lb 10oz floury white potatoes, wiped clean
100g/3½oz/¾ cup toasted hazelnuts or cobnuts, roughly chopped, to serve
2 egg yolks
15g/½oz/3½ tbsp vegetarian Parmesan, finely grated, plus extra to serve
225–280g/8–10oz/1¾–generous 2 cups plain/all-purpose flour
1 tsp baking powder
¼ tsp grated nutmeg
½ tsp sea salt, plus extra to season
150g/5½oz curly kale, tough stalks removed
freshly ground black pepper

Rosemary butter sauce
100g/3½oz/scant ½ cup butter
2 large garlic cloves, finely chopped
1 tbsp finely chopped fresh rosemary

Preheat the oven to 200°C/400°F/Gas 6. Bake both types of potatoes for 50 minutes – 1 hour until tender.

While the potatoes are baking, place the hazelnuts on a baking sheet and toast in the bottom of the oven for 12 minutes or until starting to colour.

Cut the baked potatoes in half and scoop out the flesh into a large mixing bowl. Mash with a fork until smooth and leave to cool. (Don't waste the skins – return them to the oven to crisp up for about 15 minutes.) Add the egg yolks and Parmesan to the potatoes, then gradually add the smaller quantity of flour with the baking powder, nutmeg and ½ teaspoon salt to make a soft dough. Add more flour, if needed. The dough should still be a little sticky but not wet; take care not to overwork the mixture or the gnocchi will be tough.

To cook, bring a large pan of salted water to the boil, take a small piece of the dough and put it in the water to test whether it holds together – add a bit more flour if it crumbles. Divide the dough into 6 pieces. Take one piece and roll it out on a floured work surface into a sausage, 2cm/¾in in diameter, then slice into 1.5cm/⅝in pillows. Place on a lined and floured baking sheet and repeat with the rest of the dough.

Return the water in the pan to a rolling boil and cook the gnocchi in batches of about 10 at a time for 2–3 minutes – they are ready when they float to the surface. Using a slotted spoon, scoop out the gnocchi and keep warm in a dish in a low oven.

Just before the gnocchi are ready, steam the kale for 3 minutes, or until just tender, and make the butter sauce. Heat the butter, garlic and rosemary over a low heat until melted, then season.

To serve, divide the kale between 4 large, shallow bowls. Top with the gnocchi and pour the garlicky butter over. Finish with a sprinkling of hazelnuts and extra grated Parmesan. You could serve the crisp potato skins by the side or break them into shards and place on top with the hazelnuts. If that's a bit carb-heavy for you, then the crisps will keep for a day or so.

Festive gathering

MENU
Serves 4

∘∘

Chestnut, blue cheese and cranberry galette

∘∘

Creamy leek sauce

∘∘

Spiced red cabbage

∘∘

Sprouts with smoked chilli butter

∘∘

Crushed roast potatoes with rosemary

Every Christmas spread should have a centrepiece at its heart and this meal is no exception: the galette, filled with layers of onions and chestnuts, roasted butternut squash, blue cheese and cranberries, with a final smattering of toasted walnuts, ticks all the right boxes. The beauty of this menu is that many of the dishes can be part-made in advance to relieve the pressures on the day, including the pastry and filling for the galette; the spiced red cabbage; and the smoked chilli butter for the sprouts. You don't have to peel the potatoes, either! The Parsnip, Apple and Potato Soup (see page 168) or Red Chicory Salad (see page 174) would both make perfect starters.

Chestnut, blue cheese and cranberry galette

Preparation time: 30 minutes, plus chilling and resting | Cooking time: 1 hour

400g/14oz (prepared weight) peeled
    butternut squash, cut into chunks
2½ tbsp olive oil
3 onions, thinly sliced
3 large garlic cloves, finely chopped
2 tsp balsamic vinegar
2 tsp fresh thyme leaves or 1 tsp dried
2 tsp finely chopped rosemary
225g/9oz whole cooked chestnuts,
    roughly chopped
2 tbsp crème fraîche
175g/6oz/scant 2 cups cranberries
2 tbsp caster/superfine sugar
100g/3½oz vegetarian Stilton, broken
    into chunks
1 egg, lightly beaten, for brushing
40g/1½oz/generous ⅓ cup toasted
    chopped walnuts
salt and freshly ground black pepper

Pastry
100g/3½oz/¾ cup plain/all-purpose flour,
    plus extra for dusting
100g/3½oz/¾ cup wholemeal/whole-
    wheat flour
125g/4½oz/generous ½ cup cold
    butter, cubed

First, make the pastry. Mix together the flour and a pinch of salt in a mixing bowl. Using your fingertips, gently rub in the butter until it forms coarse breadcrumbs. Stir in 1½–2 tablespoons cold water with a fork, then press the mixture together to form the pastry into a disc. Wrap in cling film/plastic wrap and chill for 30 minutes.

Meanwhile, preheat the oven to 210°C/415°F/Gas 6–7. Roast the squash in 1 tablespoon of the oil for 20 minutes or until tender. Set aside to cool.

To make the pie filling, heat the remaining oil in a frying pan over a medium-low heat, add the onion and cook for 15 minutes, stirring, until softened and starting to colour. Add the garlic and cook, stirring, for another 1 minute. Increase the heat to medium, add the vinegar and cook for another 5 minutes, stirring, until the onions have slightly caramelized. Remove a third of the onions from the pan and purée using a stick/immersion blender until smooth. Return the puréed onions to the pan along with the herbs, chestnuts and crème fraîche and warm briefly. Season and leave to cool.

Meanwhile, put the cranberries and sugar in a saucepan over a low heat and stir until the sugar dissolves. Increase the heat slightly and cook until the sugar starts to turn syrupy, about 3 minutes. Leave to cool.

Line a large baking sheet with baking paper. On a well-floured surface, roll out the pastry to a round, about 33cm/13in in diameter, and neaten the edges. Carefully lift the pastry onto the lined baking sheet. Spoon the cooled onion mixture onto the pastry, leaving a 2.5cm/1in border. Top with the roasted squash and the cheese. Fold the edges of the pastry over the filling, leaving the top open. Chill for 20 minutes.

Meanwhile, preheat the oven to 200°C/400°F/Gas 6.

Brush the pastry with beaten egg and bake for 30 minutes. Spoon the cranberries on top, then return to the oven and bake for another 15 minutes or until the pastry is cooked and golden. Remove from the oven and leave to sit for 5 minutes before serving sprinkled with the walnuts.

Creamy leek sauce

Preparation time: 10 minutes | Cooking time: 5 minutes

4 leeks, thinly sliced
4 tbsp crème fraîche or dairy-free cream
1 tsp vegetable stock/bouillon powder
salt and freshly ground black pepper

Steam the leeks for 4–5 minutes, until just tender. Drain to remove any excess water and transfer to a jug or beaker. Add 100ml/3½fl oz/scant ½ cup just-boiled water, the crème fraiche and bouillon powder, then blend using a stick/immersion blender until almost smooth (you may need to do this in 2 batches and you can use a regular blender, if preferred). Add more water, if necessary, to make a thick and creamy sauce. Season with salt and pepper to taste .

Crushed roast potatoes with rosemary

Preparation time: 10 minutes | Cooking time: 1 hour 10 minutes

1.2kg/2lb 12oz smallish, evenly sized waxy potatoes, such as Charlottes, skins left on and scrubbed
2 tbsp olive oil
40g/1½oz/3 tbsp butter or dairy-free alternative
2 long rosemary sprigs, broken into small sprigs
sea salt flakes and freshly ground black pepper

Preheat the oven to 210°C/415°F/Gas 6–7. Boil the potatoes in salted water for 12–15 minutes until almost tender, then drain well. Return the potatoes to the warm pan, add the oil and turn to coat.

Tip the potatoes into a large roasting pan, make a long, shallow cut in the top of each potato, then use the back of a fork or potato masher to crush the tops – the potatoes should keep their shapes with the top halves just split open. Spread the potatoes out in a single layer.

Put a small knob of butter on top of each potato and season with sea salt flakes and black pepper. Roast for 30 minutes, then remove from the oven and insert 2 small sprigs of rosemary into the crushed top of each potato. Roast for another 20–25 minutes or until crisp and golden.

Sprouts with smoked chilli butter

Preparation time: 5 minutes, plus 5/25 minutes for the butter | Cooking time: 5 minutes

400g/14oz sprouts, trimmed, large ones cut
    with a cross in the base
½ quantity Smoked Chilli Butter
    (see page 130)
50g/1¾oz/scant ½ cup pecans
juice of ½ lemon, or to taste
salt and freshly ground black pepper

Cook the sprouts in boiling salted water for 4 minutes or until just tender. Drain and return to the pan.

Meanwhile, toast the pecans in a large dry frying pan over a medium-low heat, turning once, for 4 minutes or until they smell toasted and start to colour. Roughly chop and set aside.

Add the smoked chilli butter to the hot cooked sprouts. Add the lemon juice, season with salt and pepper, to taste, and turn until coated. Serve the sprouts with the toasted pecans scattered over the top.

. . . .
PART-TIME VARIATION
Bacon Swap the Smoked Chilli Butter for Smoky Bacon Butter (see page 130).

Spiced red cabbage

Preparation time: 10 minutes | Cooking time: 35 minutes

1 tbsp sunflower oil
15g/½oz/1 tbsp butter or dairy-free alternative
1 red onion, thinly sliced
½ tsp ground allspice
¼ tsp caraway seeds
400g/14oz red cabbage, shredded
1 Bramley apple, skin left on, cored and
    coarsely grated
2 tbsp apple cider vinegar
1 tbsp soft light brown sugar
salt and freshly ground black pepper

Heat the oil and butter in a saucepan with a lid over a medium heat, add the onion and cook, stirring, for 5 minutes. Add the spices and then the cabbage, apple, vinegar and sugar, stirring until the sugar dissolves. Season generously.

Bring almost to the boil, then reduce the heat to low, cover, and simmer for 30 minutes, stirring occasionally, until the cabbage is tender. Remove the lid for the last 5 minutes if there is too much liquid in the base of the pan. Serve warm or at room temperature.

Index

aioli, almond 56

alfalfa sprouts
watercress, pink grapefruit and quinoa salad 31

almonds
orange and pomegranate salad with mint and lime 125
roasted carrot and couscous salad with chimichurri 154
Spanish-style baked beans with almond aioli 56

apples
parsnip, apple and potato soup with winter pesto 168
pot-roasted cauliflower in cider with apples 137
red chicory salad with honey pecans 174
spiced red cabbage 201

artichokes
broad bean humous with artichokes and pitta crisps 26

asparagus
chargrilled asparagus with wild garlic mash 42
rejuvenating coconut and spinach broth 20
spring vegetable fritto misto with saffron mayo 44
springtime Korean rice bowl 50
tomato bulgur with raw asparagus salad and mint yogurt 28

aubergines
aubergine and fresh tomato curry 84
aubergine pide 95
charred aubergine salad 104
roasted ratatouille with pasta 90
smoky aubergine chilli 142
Thai aubergines with sunflower seed raita 71

avocados
avocado, pea and mint pasta 108
barbecued baby carrots with avocado and ginger 105
beer-battered tofu tacos with pea crema 86
chipotle-baked eggs with herb salsa 170
eggs, avocado and black beans with fresh tomato salsa 66

green gazpacho 37
watercress, pink grapefruit and quinoa salad 31

beans
black bean noodles with purple sprouting broccoli 30
broad bean humous with artichokes and pitta crisps 26
chipotle-baked eggs with herb salsa 170
eggs, avocado and black beans with fresh tomato salsa 66
harissa-roasted new potatoes with beans and halloumi 54
leek and white bean soup with roast garlic oil 22
new-season potato and watercress salad 41
roasted broccoli and squash with smashed beans 128
smoky aubergine chilli 142
smoky beans 124
Spanish-style baked beans with almond aioli 56
sweetcorn polenta with roast peppers and beans 99
Turkish-style spiced pinto beans 190

beetroot
beetroot spaghetti with goat's cheese and walnuts 132
beetroot tarts with goat's cheese and dukkah 146
parsnip latkes with beetroot horseradish cream 126
bhajis: celeriac, sesame and ginger, with coriander dipping sauce 164

black beans
black bean noodles with purple sprouting broccoli 30
chipotle-baked eggs with herb salsa 170
eggs, avocado and black beans with fresh tomato salsa 66
black rice, pineapple, mint and tofu salad 162

bread
aubergine pide 95
autumn kale Caesar salad 152
baked halloumi with red mojo sauce 70

bread, kale and smoked paprika frittata 121
broccoli, lemon crumbs and crispy capers with linguine 52
chargrilled courgettes on garlic toast with parsley relish 96
roti with spinach saag and paneer 34–5
salt-cured carrot lox on rye 64
Spanish-style baked beans with almond aioli 56
spiced-leek flatbreads with mint raita 46
watermelon, pitta and goat's cheese salad 72
winter white pizza 186–8

broad beans
broad bean humous with artichokes and pitta crisps 26
green minestrone with wild garlic pesto 24
new-season potato and watercress salad 41

broccoli
baked eggs with spring greens 23
black bean noodles with purple sprouting broccoli 30
broccoli, lemon crumbs and crispy capers with linguine 52
chickpea tofu with broccoli and ginger miso dressing 180
pho with greens and pickled turnip 148
roasted broccoli and squash with smashed beans 128
smoked chilli butter greens with tagliatelle 130
spring vegetable fritto misto with saffron mayo 44

Brussels sprouts
sprouts with smoked chilli butter 201
winter green noodles with tempeh crumbs 182

bulgar wheat
autumn squash pilaf with spinach yogurt sauce 155
tomato bulgur with raw asparagus salad and mint yogurt 28

cabbage see also cavolo nero; kale

autumn kale Caesar salad 152
baked eggs with spring greens 23
crumb-coated mushroom burgers
    with root slaw 192
pho with greens and pickled turnip
    148
red chicory salad with honey pecans
    174
smoked chilli butter greens with
    tagliatelle 130
spiced red cabbage 201
spring green and leek filo pie 40
winter green noodles with tempeh
    crumbs 182

capers
broccoli, lemon crumbs and crispy
    capers with linguine 52
pot-roasted cauliflower in cider with
    apples 137
salt-cured carrot lox on rye 64
sesame empanada pie 106
summer herb cheese 94

carrots
barbecued baby carrots with
    avocado and ginger 105
carrot, ginger and lentil soup with
    carrot crisps 116
crumb-coated mushroom burgers
    with root slaw 192
gado gado summer platter with
    wonton chips 75
mango, carrot and cardamom lassi
    79
roasted carrot and couscous salad
    with chimichurri 154
salt-cured carrot lox on rye 64
springtime Korean rice bowl 50

cashew nuts
black rice, pineapple, mint and tofu
    salad 162
green gazpacho 37

cauliflower
baked cauliflower cheese risotto
    134–5
cauliflower, coconut and lemongrass
    soup 118
pot-roasted cauliflower in cider with
    apples 137
roasted one-pan sweet potato hash
    184
sesame cauliflower noodles with
    tahini sauce 89

cavolo nero
baked cavolo nero, leek and porcini

pasta 193
polenta bowl with cavolo nero and
    chestnut crumbs 150
warm lentil salad with roasted pears,
    blue cheese and pecans 176
winter white pizza 186–8

celeriac
celeriac, sesame and ginger bhajis
    with coriander dipping sauce
    164
slow-cooked pulled celeriac with
    roast garlic cream 178–9

chard
rainbow chard with lemon butter
    141
Sri Lankan-style jackfruit curry with
    rainbow chard 144
weekday dahl 172

cheese
autumn kale Caesar salad 152
baked cauliflower cheese risotto
    134–5
baked halloumi with red mojo sauce
    70
beetroot spaghetti with goat's
    cheese and walnuts 132
beetroot tarts with goat's cheese
    and dukkah 146
chestnut, blue cheese and cranberry
    galette 197
courgette koftas in vine tomato
    sauce 98
green rice and peas 48
harissa-roasted new potatoes with
    beans and halloumi 54
pumpkin, chickpea and barley soup
    166
roasted broccoli and squash with
    smashed beans 128
roti with spinach saag and paneer
    34–5
Spanish-style baked beans with
    almond aioli 56
spiced-leek flatbreads with mint
    raita 46
spring green and leek filo pie 40
summer herb cheese 94
sweet potato tortilla 49
warm lentil salad with roasted pears,
    blue cheese and pecans 176
watermelon, pitta and goat's cheese
    salad 72
winter white pizza 186–8

chestnuts

chestnut, blue cheese and cranberry
    galette 197
polenta bowl with cavolo nero and
    chestnut crumbs 150

chickpea flour
chickpea pancakes with coriander
    yogurt 83
chickpea tofu with broccoli and
    ginger miso dressing 180

chickpeas
autumn kale Caesar salad 152
broad bean humous with artichokes
    and pitta crisps 26
pumpkin, chickpea and barley soup
    166
roasted one-pan sweet potato hash
    184
roasted spiced tofu with corn chaat
    68
chicory: red chicory salad with
    honey pecans 174
chilli: smoky aubergine 142

coconut cream
Thai aubergines with sunflower seed
    raita 71

coconut milk
black rice, pineapple, mint and tofu
    salad 162
cauliflower, coconut and lemongrass
    soup 118
rejuvenating coconut and spinach
    broth 20
Sri Lankan-style jackfruit curry with
    rainbow chard 144

coconut water
mango, carrot and cardamom lassi 79

courgettes
chargrilled courgettes on garlic toast
    with parsley relish 96
courgette koftas in vine tomato
    sauce 98
jackfruit kebabs with tahini yogurt
    sauce 101
roasted ratatouille with pasta 90
warm green bean and courgette
    salad 92

couscous
roasted carrot and couscous salad
    with chimichurri 154
Turkish-style spiced pinto beans 190
cranberries: chestnut, blue cheese
    and cranberry galette 197

cream cheese
salt-cured carrot lox on rye 64

summer herb cheese 94

cucumber
crispy mushroom pancakes with
hoisin sauce 119
gado gado summer platter with
wonton chips 75
roasted spiced tofu with corn chaat
68
seaweed salad with pickled ginger
80
watermelon, pitta and goat's cheese
salad 72
curries: aubergine and fresh tomato
curry 84
Sri Lankan-style jackfruit curry with
rainbow chard 144
Thai aubergines with sunflower seed
raita 71
weekday dahl 172

dahl: weekday 172

eggs
autumn kale Caesar salad 152
baked eggs with spring greens 23
bread, kale and smoked paprika
frittata 121
chipotle-baked eggs with herb salsa
170
corn and tofu fritters with tomato
herb relish 67
eggs, avocado and black beans with
fresh tomato salsa 66
gado gado summer platter with
wonton chips 75
Japanese-style omelette with
summer leaves 82
Japanese-style scrambled eggs with
rice 167
pak choi, miso and smoked-tofu
ramen 58
parsnip latkes with beetroot
horseradish cream 126
sesame empanada pie 106
spring green and leek filo pie 40
springtime Korean rice bowl 50
sweet potato tortilla 49
empanada: sesame 106

fennel
roasted fennel 'paella' with almond
aioli 88

gazpacho, green 37

gnocchi: sweet potato, with butter
sauce and hazelnuts 194

grapefruit
watercress, pink grapefruit and
quinoa salad 31

green beans
gado gado summer platter with
wonton chips 75
sweetcorn polenta with roast
peppers and beans 99
warm green bean and courgette
salad 92

hazelnuts
pot-roasted cauliflower in cider with
apples 137
sweet potato gnocchi with butter
sauce and hazelnuts 194

jackfruit
jackfruit kebabs with tahini yogurt
sauce 101
Sri Lankan-style jackfruit curry with
rainbow chard 144
Japanese-style omelette with
summer leaves 82
Japanese-style scrambled eggs with
rice 167

Jerusalem artichokes
winter white pizza 186–8

kale
autumn kale Caesar salad 152
black bean noodles with purple
sprouting broccoli 30
black rice, pineapple, mint and tofu
salad 162
bread, kale and smoked paprika
frittata 121
pho with greens and pickled turnip
148
warm lentil salad with roasted pears,
blue cheese and pecans 176
winter green noodles with tempeh
crumbs 182

larb: mushroom noodle 131
lassi: mango, carrot and cardamom 79
latkes: parsnip, with beetroot
horseradish cream 126

leeks
baked cavolo nero, leek and porcini
pasta 193
creamy leek sauce 200

green minestrone with wild garlic
pesto 24
leek and white bean soup with roast
garlic oil 22
spiced-leek flatbreads with mint
raita 46
spring green and leek filo pie 40

lemons
autumn squash pilaf with spinach
yogurt sauce 155
baked halloumi with red mojo sauce
70
broad bean humous with artichokes
and pitta crisps 26
broccoli, lemon crumbs and crispy
capers with linguine 52
cauliflower, coconut and lemongrass
soup 118
rainbow chard with lemon butter 141
roasted broccoli and squash with
smashed beans 128
tomato tarts with preserved lemon
relish 110
Turkish-style spiced pinto beans 190

lentils
carrot, ginger and lentil soup with
carrot crisps 116
courgette koftas in vine tomato
sauce 98
rich lentil ragu 189
warm lentil salad with roasted pears,
blue cheese and pecans 176
weekday dahl 172

lettuce see also salads
chargrilled lettuce with miso
dressing 105
green rice and peas 48

limes
beer-battered tofu tacos with pea
crema 86
corn with chilli and lime 104
gado gado summer platter with
wonton chips 75
orange and pomegranate salad with
mint and lime 125
pho with greens and pickled turnip
148
radicchio with Thai flavours 160
Thai aubergines with sunflower seed
raita 71

menu ideas: barbecue feast 100–5
brunch 120–5
festive gathering 196–201

meal for a gathering 136–41
spring lunch 36–41
summer picnic platter 74–9

milk
baked cavolo nero, leek and porcini
pasta 193
minestrone: green, with wild garlic
pesto 24

miso
chargrilled lettuce with miso
dressing 105
chickpea tofu with broccoli and
ginger miso dressing 180
dairy-free cacio e pepe 53
pak choi, miso and smoked-tofu
ramen 58
rich lentil ragu 189

mushrooms
baked cavolo nero, leek and porcini
pasta 193
crispy mushroom pancakes with
hoisin sauce 119
crumb-coated mushroom burgers
with root slaw 192
mushroom noodle larb 131
pak choi, miso and smoked-tofu
ramen 58
pho with greens and pickled turnip
148
springtime Korean rice bowl 50
winter white pizza 186–8

noodles
black bean noodles with purple
sprouting broccoli 30
mushroom noodle larb 131
pak choi, miso and smoked-tofu
ramen 58
pho with greens and pickled turnip
148
sesame cauliflower noodles with
tahini sauce 89
winter green noodles with tempeh
crumbs 182

nuts
baked cauliflower cheese risotto
134–5
beetroot spaghetti with goat's
cheese and walnuts 132
black rice, pineapple, mint and tofu
salad 162
chestnut, blue cheese and cranberry
galette 197
chickpea tofu with broccoli and

ginger miso dressing 180
dairy-free cacio e pepe 53
green gazpacho 37
orange and pomegranate salad with
mint and lime 125
pot-roasted cauliflower in cider with
apples 137
radicchio with Thai flavours 160
red chicory salad with honey pecans
174
roasted carrot and couscous salad
with chimichurri 154
Spanish-style baked beans with
almond aioli 56
sprouts with smoked chilli butter
201
sweet potato gnocchi with butter
sauce and hazelnuts 194
tomato tarts with preserved lemon
relish 110
warm lentil salad with roasted pears,
blue cheese and pecans 176
winter white pizza 186–8

oats
pot-roasted cauliflower in cider with
apples 137

olives
roasted ratatouille with pasta 90
sesame empanada pie 106
omelette: Japanese-style, with
summer leaves 82

onions
eggs, avocado and black beans with
fresh tomato salsa 66
harissa-roasted new potatoes with
beans and halloumi 54
jackfruit kebabs with tahini yogurt
sauce 101
pot-roasted cauliflower in cider with
apples 137
red onion tarte tatin with pine nuts
32
roasted one-pan sweet potato hash
184
roasted ratatouille with pasta 90
sesame empanada pie 106
warm green bean and courgette
salad 92
warm lentil salad with roasted pears,
blue cheese and pecans 176

oranges
orange and pomegranate salad with
mint and lime 125

slow-cooked pulled celeriac with
roast garlic cream 178–9

parsnips
parsnip, apple and potato soup with
winter pesto 168
parsnip latkes with beetroot
horseradish cream 126
roasted one-pan sweet potato hash
184

pasta
avocado, pea and mint pasta 108
baked cavolo nero, leek and porcini
pasta 193
beetroot spaghetti with goat's
cheese and walnuts 132
broccoli, lemon crumbs and crispy
capers with linguine 52
dairy-free cacio e pepe 53
green minestrone with wild garlic
pesto 24
roasted ratatouille with pasta 90
smoked chilli butter greens with
tagliatelle 130
peanut butter: gado gado summer
platter with wonton chips 75

peanuts
chickpea tofu with broccoli and
ginger miso dressing 180
radicchio with Thai flavours 160

pearl barley
pumpkin, chickpea and barley soup
166

pears
warm lentil salad with roasted pears,
blue cheese and pecans 176

peas
avocado, pea and mint pasta 108
beer-battered tofu tacos with pea
crema 86
green rice and peas 48

pecans
red chicory salad with honey pecans
174
sprouts with smoked chilli butter
201
warm lentil salad with roasted pears,
blue cheese and pecans 176

peppers
aubergine pide 95
baked halloumi with red mojo sauce
70
black rice, pineapple, mint and tofu
salad 162

chipotle-baked eggs with herb salsa
170
jackfruit kebabs with tahini yogurt
sauce 101
mushroom noodle larb 131
roasted fennel 'paella' with almond
aioli 88
roasted ratatouille with pasta 90
sesame empanada pie 106
smoky aubergine chilli 142
sweetcorn polenta with roast
peppers and beans 99
pho with greens and pickled turnip
148

pies and tarts
beetroot tarts with goat's cheese
and dukkah 146
chestnut, blue cheese and cranberry
galette 197
red onion tarte tatin with pine nuts
32
sesame empanada pie 106
spring green and leek filo pie 40
tomato tarts with preserved lemon
relish 110

pineapple
black rice, pineapple, mint and tofu
salad 162
radicchio with Thai flavours 160

pistachios
tomato tarts with preserved lemon
relish 110
pizza: winter white 186–8
polenta bowl with cavolo nero and
chestnut crumbs 150

pomegranate
orange and pomegranate salad with
mint and lime 125

potatoes
baked eggs with spring greens 23
cauliflower, coconut and lemongrass
soup 118
chargrilled asparagus with wild garlic
mash 42
crushed roast potatoes with
rosemary 200
gado gado summer platter with
wonton chips 75
green minestrone with wild garlic
pesto 24
harissa-roasted new potatoes with
beans and halloumi 54
new-season potato and watercress
salad 41

parsnip, apple and potato soup with
winter pesto 168
Scandi-style potato gratin 140
spiced-leek flatbreads with mint
raita 46
sweet potato gnocchi with butter
sauce and hazelnuts 194
pumpkin, chickpea and barley soup
166

quinoa
watercress, pink grapefruit and
quinoa salad 31

radicchio with Thai flavours 160
radishes
eggs, avocado and black beans with
fresh tomato salsa 66
gado gado summer platter with
wonton chips 75
seaweed salad with pickled ginger
80
watermelon, pitta and goat's cheese
salad 72

rainbow chard
rainbow chard with lemon butter
141
Sri Lankan-style jackfruit curry with
rainbow chard 144
ramen: pak choi, miso and smoked-
tofu 58
ratatouille: roasted, with pasta 90
red chicory salad with honey pecans
174

rice
baked cauliflower cheese risotto
134–5
black rice, pineapple, mint and tofu
salad 162
green rice and peas 48
Japanese-style scrambled eggs with
rice 167
roasted fennel 'paella' with almond
aioli 88
seaweed salad with pickled ginger
80
springtime Korean rice bowl 50
roti with spinach saag and paneer
34–5

salads
autumn kale Caesar salad 152
black rice, pineapple, mint and tofu
salad 162

charred aubergine salad 104
new-season potato and watercress
salad 41
orange and pomegranate salad with
mint and lime 125
red chicory salad with honey pecans
174
roasted carrot and couscous salad
with chimichurri 154
seaweed salad with pickled ginger
80
tomato bulgur with raw asparagus
salad and mint yogurt 28
warm green bean and courgette
salad 92
warm lentil salad with roasted pears,
blue cheese and pecans 176
watercress, pink grapefruit and
quinoa salad 31
watermelon, pitta and goat's cheese
salad 72
samphire: spring vegetable fritto
misto with saffron mayo 44
Scandi-style potato gratin 140
seaweed salad with pickled ginger 80

soups
carrot, ginger and lentil soup with
carrot crisps 116
cauliflower, coconut and lemongrass
soup 118
green gazpacho 37
green minestrone with wild garlic
pesto 24
leek and white bean soup with roast
garlic oil 22
pak choi, miso and smoked-tofu
ramen 58
parsnip, apple and potato soup with
winter pesto 168
pho with greens and pickled turnip
148
pumpkin, chickpea and barley soup
166
rejuvenating coconut and spinach
broth 20
Spanish-style baked beans with
almond aioli 56

spinach
autumn squash pilaf with spinach
yogurt sauce 155
chickpea pancakes with coriander
yogurt 83
green gazpacho 37
Japanese-style scrambled eggs with

rice 167
rejuvenating coconut and spinach
  broth 20
roti with spinach saag and paneer
  34–5
sesame cauliflower noodles with
  tahini sauce 89
springtime Korean rice bowl 50
Turkish-style spiced pinto beans 190

squash
autumn squash pilaf with spinach
  yogurt sauce 155
chestnut, blue cheese and cranberry
  galette 197
roasted broccoli and squash with
  smashed beans 128
smoky aubergine chilli 142
Sri Lankan-style jackfruit curry with
  rainbow chard 144

sugar snap peas
gado gado summer platter with
  wonton chips 75
tomato bulgur with raw asparagus
  salad and mint yogurt 28

sweet potatoes
roasted one-pan sweet potato hash
  184
smoky aubergine chilli 142
sweet potato gnocchi with butter
  sauce and hazelnuts 194
sweet potato tortilla 49

sweetcorn
corn and tofu fritters with tomato
  herb relish 67
corn with chilli and lime 104
roasted spiced tofu with corn chaat
  68
sweetcorn polenta with roast
  peppers and beans 99

tarts see also pies and tarts
tempeh: winter green noodles with
  tempeh crumbs 182
Thai aubergines with sunflower seed
  raita 71

tofu
beer-battered tofu tacos with pea
  crema 86
black bean noodles with purple
  sprouting broccoli 30
black rice, pineapple, mint and tofu
  salad 162
chickpea tofu with broccoli and
  ginger miso dressing 180

corn and tofu fritters with tomato
  herb relish 67
gado gado summer platter with
  wonton chips 75
pak choi, miso and smoked-tofu
  ramen 58
roasted one-pan sweet potato hash
  184
roasted spiced tofu with corn chaat
  68

tomatoes
aubergine and fresh tomato curry 84
aubergine pide 95
beer-battered tofu tacos with pea
  crema 86
charred aubergine salad 104
chipotle-baked eggs with herb salsa
  170
corn and tofu fritters with tomato
  herb relish 67
courgette koftas in vine tomato
  sauce 98
eggs, avocado and black beans with
  fresh tomato salsa 66
harissa-roasted new potatoes with
  beans and halloumi 54
pumpkin, chickpea and barley soup
  166
rich lentil ragu 189
roasted ratatouille with pasta 90
sesame empanada pie 106
smoky aubergine chilli 142
smoky beans 124
Spanish-style baked beans with
  almond aioli 56
sweetcorn polenta with roast
  peppers and beans 99
tomato bulgur with raw asparagus
  salad and mint yogurt 28
tomato tarts with preserved lemon
  relish 110
Turkish-style spiced pinto beans 190
warm green bean and courgette
  salad 92
Turkish-style spiced pinto beans 190

turnips
crispy mushroom pancakes with
  hoisin sauce 119
crumb-coated mushroom burgers
  with root slaw 192
pho with greens and pickled turnip
  148
springtime Korean rice bowl 50

walnuts
baked cauliflower cheese risotto
  134–5
beetroot spaghetti with goat's
  cheese and walnuts 132
chestnut, blue cheese and cranberry
  galette 197
dairy-free cacio e pepe 53
winter white pizza 186–8

watercress
green gazpacho 37
new-season potato and watercress
  salad 41
sweet potato tortilla 49
watercress, pink grapefruit and
  quinoa salad 31
watermelon, pitta and goat's cheese
  salad 72
wonton chips 78

yogurt
autumn squash pilaf with spinach
  yogurt sauce 155
baked eggs with spring greens 23
celeriac, sesame and ginger bhajis
  with coriander dipping sauce
  164
chickpea pancakes with coriander
  yogurt 83
crumb-coated mushroom burgers
  with root slaw 192
jackfruit kebabs with tahini yogurt
  sauce 101
mango, carrot and cardamom lassi
  79
orange and pomegranate salad with
  mint and lime 125
roasted one-pan sweet potato hash
  184
roasted spiced tofu with corn chaat
  68
tomato bulgur with raw asparagus
  salad and mint yogurt 28
weekday dahl 172

Acknowledgements

It has been such a joy to write this book. From creating the original concept, to forming a list of recipes, testing and writing, seeing the recipes jump to life at the photoshoots, and finally watching the book come together in the design and layouts – I have loved every minute of it! By my side at each stage has been a team of super-talented, super-experienced colleagues and I would like to thank them all:

Firstly, a heartfelt thank you to managing and commissioning editor, Dan Hurst, for commissioning me, for creating a dream-team and for overseeing this book, ensuring everything ran smoothly and seamlessly.

Thank you, too, to editor Emily Preece-Morrison – the epitome of calm and efficiency, not to mention more than impressive editing skills.

Liz and Max Haarala Hamilton photographed the recipes in the first book, and I was so delighted that they were commissioned for the second. What a team! Their studio is just the right balance of effortless calm and creativity – I love the shots, thank you so much!

I've been so lucky to have master food stylist, Valerie Berry, prepare the recipes so expertly for the food shots. Thank you, Valerie, for making everything look so beautiful. The same can be said of stylist, Linda Berlin, whose selection of props enhanced the look of the dishes.

This has been my ninth book (coincidentally my lucky number!) for my publisher Watkins/Nourish and it has been an honour – thank you so much for your continued support. The editorial, sales and marketing teams may have changed over the years, but I'm hugely grateful for giving me the opportunity to write this sequel to *Part-Time Vegetarian*. Thank you to Fiona Robertson and Vicky Hartley, as well as Georgina Hewitt for creating the initial design of the book and to Glen Wilkins for taking up the mantle.

Cookery books are very much a team effort, and it has been such a privilege to work with you all.